In Love But Worlds Apart

*Insights, questions, and tips for the
intercultural couple*

G. Shelling and J. Fraser-Smith

authorHOUSE®

AuthorHouse™
1663 Liberty Drive, Suite 200
Bloomington, IN 47403
www.authorhouse.com
Phone: 1-800-839-8640

© 2008 G. Shelling and J. Fraser-Smith. All rights reserved.

*No part of this book may be reproduced, stored in a retrieval system, or
transmitted by any means without the written permission of the authors.*

First published by AuthorHouse 6/2/2008

ISBN: 978-1-4343-8116-3 (sc)

Library of Congress Control Number: 2008903053

Printed in the United States of America
Bloomington, Indiana

This book is printed on acid-free paper.

Cartoon drawings: Bethany Bell
Art designs: J. Fraser-Smith
Cover design: Susan Wayman

Scripture taken from the HOLY BIBLE, NEW INTERNATIONAL VERSION. Copyright ©
1973, 1978, 1984 International Bible Society. Used by permission of Zondervan Bible Publishers.

This book is dedicated to...

My husband, Ted,
my son, Timothy,
– G.S.

my husband, Keith,
Caroline and Mike,
Andrew and Hege
and Katie.
– J.R.F-S.

Acknowledgments

Without the privilege of having had many friends and acquaintances, clients, and neighbors literally from all over the world who have shared with us their joys and struggles, we could not have written this book. Specifically we would like to mention Michael and Ellen Burslem, Leiton and Lisa Chinn, Wichit and Miriam Maneevone, Helga and Dick DuMosch, David and Helga Stewart, and Sam and Ruth Thiagarajan; whose exemplary intercultural marriages have inspired us and many others. Special thanks go also to Ngaire Jehle for encouraging author J. Fraser-Smith to further an interest in the subject of intercultural marriage. We would also like to recognize Dr. Mary Lou Codman-Wilson, whose wisdom in the journal Bridges with its sensitivity to the dynamics of culture challenged both authors toward further reflection.

We are especially grateful for the following who labored hard with us and for us by reading the manuscript, or parts of it, and who gave us valuable input (in alphabetical order): Nezihat Bakar, Claudia Carrera, Dr. Heidi Chew, Dr. Arthur Domig, Andrew Fraser-Smith, Kate Fraser-Smith, John Gary, Mao Gheraieri, Rebecca Honts, Pauline McGibbon, Bill Perry, Jo Saxton, Timothy Shelling, Caroline Stoodley, Dr. Anh Van Tran, Dr. Ann Yeardley, and Rebecca Zillinger. Also special thanks to all our friends and relatives who have cheered us on and supported us in many other ways along the way.

Contents

For Whom We Wrote This Book, And Why

Many couples who are about to embark on a long-term relationship think all they need is that warm feeling of love and maybe a little compromise here and there, and that everything then will fall into place. They say that the future will take care of itself. But couples who have gone this journey tell us that this just is not enough, *especially* couples whose partners hail from two different cultures or countries!

Many books have been written about gender differences and about issues that interracial couples face. This book concerns itself with neither, but rather, with *cultural* differences in *intercultural* couples. By that we mean two or more different sets of cultural values, beliefs, heart connections, tastes, language, goals and practices, which a man and a woman bring with them into the relationship who come from two different cultures or countries.

Differences between the modern Western mindset (such as that of the European and North American) and the non-Western one, such as those of Asia, Africa, Eurasia, the Middle East and the Far East may seem more obvious to some. Yet huge cultural differences can also exist between partners who grew up *within* the West, especially among those whose ancestors or influences stem from two totally different cultures. Class differences due to variations in financial income, education, social heritage and geography (such as the urban-rural divide) also complicate the cultural nuances all over the world.

The number of all these various combinations and their stories could reach thousands, and no adequate number of volumes could ever tell them all. However, as we gathered observations and experiences on this subject, we gleaned some themes and principles that could be applied by many of these combinations.

Intercultural couples do not always have it easy. Not only do they face the *external* challenge of prejudice and rejection by family or community, but they must also tackle the *internal* challenges related to their complex cultural differences. Such couples often turn to their families and friends for advice, but their family and friends simply do not know how to advise.

And that is why we wrote this book. Whether drawn together through physical attraction, fascination about each other's cultures or a flight from one's own culture — whatever the combination and whatever the drawing point — we believe that if intercultural partners gain understanding of themselves, their respective cultures, and of each other, then they have a chance to fulfill their dream of a successful relationship.

G. Shelling

The Source Of The Metaphor

A work of art! Where did the idea come from to call a long-term relationship between a man and woman *a work of art*?!

Working together with someone else can be deemed a work of art in itself because it draws out each person's creativity. The skill required to cooperate closely together with someone else is both work and a creation, something that came from nothing to become the setting for a life together and for any children that might arrive.

The question this book addresses is, is such an art project possible for an intercultural couple? Can they succeed? If so, how?

Cindy, a friend of mine in Cyprus asked me once, "Why am I like I am and why is he like he is? We were so happy in the UK. Our home was just as I wanted it, and he seemed to be very happy with the way things were. He seemed to fit in so well. Now we are back here in his country, and he seems to have changed. He is so much more like everyone else here. He speaks as loudly too. It is me that doesn't fit in at all now."

How can anyone explain this feeling of "fitting in" and "not fitting in?" What did this woman sense about her partner and herself, and what were these feelings that unsettled her? I needed to find a way to explain how differences of culture are embedded in us at a profound level.

In a moment of inspiration I thought of watercolor paper. Until you give it an under-wash of some color or other, it is white. A yellow ochre under-wash will give the final painting a warm hue. If the under-wash is ultramarine blue, the final painting will look very different and be quite cool.

And so it is with a cultural undertone. In one sense, everyone from a particular culture will use the same undertone which gives a sense of cohesion within the society. This does not mean that everyone is the same but that they are similar in key respects.

Reflecting further, I realized that in our youth we take in all sorts of experiences and mannerisms that sink in to the core of our beings, giving us a cultural color. This cultural under-wash on our "canvas" stays with us and is reinforced if we stay in our village or town of country, but it might be altered if we are lucky enough to live in other places as well. The trace of an accent, the messages of history, the traditions of men and women and yes, our expectations of marriage and the roles within the home give us away. It affects how we view everything, including compatibility, tolerance, and their opposites.

It is, though, very difficult to recognize our own "color." Our own cultural color prevents us from seeing things that perhaps only others are able to see. At best it reduces the options of what we *could* see, and this limit affects how we interpret the world around us. These cultural colors determine our values, which in turn prioritize what we do see.

The other aspect that is part of creating "art work" is that each partner brings to this relationship their own palette, their own brushes and size of canvas. One may prefer oils or clay or mixed media and the other plain water color. One may be a trained artist, the other an amateur. Both have had experiences of successes and failures that might affect how they wish to work together. Yet both have a lot to learn from each other and to contribute to each other.

As I discussed this with Cindy, she seemed to understand better that neither of them could completely change. I explained to her that it would take her a while to recognize his cultural "colors." Once she did, she would then be able to respond to many of their differences as merely having different viewpoints, tastes, customs, etc., instead of being right and wrong. I also challenged her to take a closer look at their clashes: Each one would have to be viewed differently according to whether it was due to a personality weakness, immaturity, or a cultural difference.

Like Cindy and her partner, if you begin an intercultural relationship, you and your partner will become more and more like artists working on one piece of art: You will always be looking for and discovering new ways to do things, developing, building on and branching out from the skills and observations you start out with. You will continue to explore your world as you see it and find appropriate ways to respond to it emotionally. As time passes, both the piece of art and you the artists will benefit from your growth as individuals.

But this does not happen automatically. Just as in a watercolor painting in which the colors sometimes shine through others, only as you collaborate honestly and openly with each other will you be able to bring about the desired results. Of course, some of the outcome will still be a surprise, but if it's one you can both accept, then why not?

J. R. Fraser-Smith

Notes to the Reader:

1. To maximize the benefit of this book, we recommend that you make two copies of Appendix I and II (both at the end of this book). Then use as directed.

2. All names have been changed for reasons of confidentiality except where full names are used.

3. Generally, when we mention "partners" or "partnership", we are referring to marriage partners, although we understand that in some cultures there are no marriage ceremonies.

4. The authors apologize for any statements that may appear as generalizations related to the culture or characteristics of specific people groups. These were unintended.

5. We would welcome your input or questions by writing to the following: inLovebutWorldsApart@yahoo.com

Chapter 1 Pairing the Partners

What kind of partner am I looking for?

An artist has a dream, a vision that inspires a piece of art so profound, so intricate, so personal, that the whole idea is quite overwhelming. The vision is so big that it cannot be done alone; it will take the artist's entire life — with someone else — to complete. Wisely, this artist seeks a partner, a fellow artist, someone with whom this great piece of art will be produced. The artist has some idea of what qualities this potential partner should have.

But how to choose? If ten potential partners line up, ready to be recruited, which should the artist choose? Will the artist make this decision alone? Or will someone else help? Or will someone else make the choice? In addition to the method of choosing, both the artist and the potential co-artists are asking the same question, namely, "What do you wish my role would be? How do you see me fitting into your dream or vision?"

A young man has a dream. A young woman has high hopes. They don't know each other, yet. They do know that what they want is something quite out of this world — a partner who will love them and will share the very best that life can offer. At this stage, they do not know that this person will indeed be worlds apart in their experiences and in their understanding of how their dreams will take shape.

Many individuals make the mistake of letting just any person of the opposite sex "sweep them off their feet," only to realize later that they wasted time, money, and energy on a relationship they had never really wanted. They simply had never bothered to ask the *role expectation* question.

Role expectations vary from person to person, of course, and so do their level of importance. To begin with, they depend on the goals and hopes a person has for a partnership or marriage. There are several possibilities of goals:

- to provide for a companion and friend

- to make sure everything necessary for living gets done that needs to be done

- to advance a family business or wealth

- to contribute to the stability of the larger community

- to enjoy a fulfilling sex life

- to control sexual urges for the safety of the community

- to create offspring (children), and to provide a safe environment for them

- to be cared for when old

- to have help in caring for the elderly and needy in the extended family

Once the seeking partner has established what these goals are, then the envisioned role of the potential partner becomes more clear. The next logical question then is, "Who will best fulfill my goals and this role?" The search can then begin.

1   To choose or to be chosen

How can you find "the one"?

First to the obvious question every single person asks: "How do I find a partner who will work best with me on this 'art project' of a life relationship?"

There are basically three ways you can find a partner for life: (1) Someone else chooses for you; (2) you choose and the other is chosen; or (3) both you and the other have a say and therefore both choose. There are many variations in each of these approaches. Here is a brief overlook of the first two, then a more detailed discussion of the third.

(a) Someone else chooses for us.

Usually in arranged marriages, families of both sons and daughters are involved in finding and choosing a partner for their children. Sometimes the family gives their grown child a number of photos and descriptions to choose from; nonetheless, such a choice is limited. Surprisingly to those in the West, such an arranged marriage could and often does lead to a healthy relationship and even a romantic one. More important than romance, however, is the fulfillment of duty and the loyalty to the marriage itself. These marriages have a good chance of survival if both partners share the same world views, religion, values, behavioral customs, and rules, and if they have a strong family support system.

(b) You choose and I am chosen.

The family gives away the bride to a man who finds her, chooses her, and asks for her hand in marriage. The expression, "She swept him off his feet," implies that she was an active seeker and that he was passively waiting to be found. Sounds romantic and glorious, doesn't it? But it isn't always. When someone chooses someone else, that someone else is chosen. Perhaps the chooser not only chooses *who*, but also *what, where, how,* and *when.*

> *I met Tom at a school function. Tom's good looks, warm charm, social standing, and intense interest left me feeling like a princess. Our first date was at a horror movie which he chose, but which I couldn't bear to watch. When we went to the mall, he picked out skimpy clothes for me to try on and wear on our next outings. One day Tom saw me conversing with a class-mate — another guy — in the school cafeteria. He was furious. The next time he saw me alone he told me that I was not allowed to spend time alone with another guy.*
>
> *– S. from USA*

3

This is a modern, western instance of this choose-or-be-chosen option, and it happens every day. Stacy realized that being chosen, as romantic as it seemed, might mean never being able to make choices as long as she remained in that relationship.

In summary, depending on which worldview and values the couple and its families come from, the partner who is chosen should ask,

- Did I choose you, or did I merely respond to your choosing me?

- Does it mean that if you choose me, I have to do as you say?

- Do I have to conform to your family expectations and culture? Or do I still have the power and freedom to choose to the extent I desire and need?

(c) We both have a say.

Most *intercultural* couples are made up of partners who choose each other. The person attracted to the other tries to invite that other person's attention through eye contact, smiles, endearing words and gifts, then hopes that the other returns those signals with similar ones. Each partner then explores if the other meets at least a few basic criteria for making the relationship a long-lasting one. Usually *romantic* love develops; that is the feeling of being special and wanted as well as the desire to make the other person feel special and wanted. Wanting to spend time together in combination with sexual arousal are considered the first indicators that *this* find might be right. Words or actions usually follow that say, "I like you a lot," and eventually, "I value and cherish you and I wish you would be mine forever." If the attraction is mutual and the appropriate signals are expressed on both sides, the relationship might turn into a commitment for life.

This mindset of "we are on our own in this choice" often ignores the fact that families and friends will be involved, whether the couple likes it or not and even if they are on the other side of the world.

2 Prioritizing your criteria

How would I know if he or she is the right one?

Assuming you have a choice, how can you know if the potential partner is right for you? To answer this question, you need your head, not just your heart.

Most people on the lookout for a life partner or spouse base their search on certain criteria important to them. However, many are not always conscious of what those criteria really are; they are overlooked or taken for granted. Besides external, physical criteria such as physique, face, hair, body language, social behavior, and so on, there are other criteria that are less visible but might be just as or more important to consider. Furthermore, finding a partner for life is not necessarily based on popular notions such as "opposites attract!"

The questions you must ask yourself include:

- Which criteria are important to me now?

- Which will be important later to me once we are married?

- Does this potential partner have the most important qualities I want in a partner?

To help you become more aware of what some of *your* criteria are, peruse the list called "My Priorities of Preference" in Appendix II. Use this list to help you get a clearer picture of what type of person you would want to spend your life with.

One caution, however, especially to those who want "all or nothing." No one will ever meet *all* the criteria. That is why it is helpful to first decide which criteria are most important to you, and to be open to sacrificing some of the less important criteria. Do this *before* you compare those criteria with the qualities of your partner.

Other considerations...

(a) ***Where can I meet and get to know this person?*** This depends on the country and culture. Most young adults meet each other for the first time in class, at work, in church, in a social club or organization, or in other formal or informal situations. In some cultures it is only polite for the man to initiate eye contact, or to begin a conversation, or to introduce himself. In others, names are never exchanged until hours into a conversation.

(b) ***What if friends or relatives introduce me to someone?*** This well-meaning service might or might not work. You don't have to feel obligated to take their suggestion, but you might have to take into consideration how to refuse appropriately in the culture where you live.

(c) ***What about Internet dating and matching services?*** In a multicultural society as in most countries in the West, Internet matching services certainly can shorten what some people consider a painstaking search. They operate on the principle of finding a match according to criteria such as income, education level, physical attributes, race, religion, astrological sign, geography, and so on. Some of these services offer an extensive check system to help partners know that the information given can be trusted. However, the matched pair would still need to meet, spend time together, and see for themselves how honest they were in their self-report, if they "connect" romantically and on a deeper level, and, of course, if they are culturally compatible with each other.

(d) *What if you are attracted to someone who turns out to have an aspect of personality or lifestyle that you really don't like?* If you hope and think that the person you have fallen in love with will change for you, don't count on it, even if he or she promises to do so. This person might change temporarily or not at all, no matter how influential you think you might be. The questions to consider include:

- What if my partner never changes in the areas that I want him to change, would I still want to stay with him?

- How will I react if my partner changes in ways that I would not want her to change?

- What if my criteria change as time goes on?

(e) *What about parents and friends who don't approve of the one you've chosen?* Their set of criteria for a partner for you might differ from yours, or you had no idea what their criteria were to begin with, or you are simply so blindly in love that you don't see what your parents or friends see. To prevent such heartache, ask for your family's input *before* the relationship "gets serious." If they are against the relationship for whatever reason and you are unable to convince them that he or she is right for you, consider the following questions: "Am I prepared to sacrifice my relationship with my parents (or friends) in order to be together with this partner?" And even more importantly, "How would they get along with him or her at future family celebrations?"

> *I had no idea that my French parents didn't wish me to get involved with someone from another country. He was intelligent, had great manners, and I assumed that his being Finnish wouldn't matter. But it did. They were afraid of losing me and that I would have to move to Finland. When they insisted I break up with him, I cried and cried. I was already in love and didn't want to lose him.*
>
> *-J. from France*

> *When I fell in love with Katje from Holland at a study seminar in another country, she said she would only marry a Christian. So I began to read her Bible and learn all about her faith. But my Muslim parents were furious when they found out about her. They threatened to disown me if I continued this relationship. I was still a student and couldn't afford to lose their support. And*

I loved them, too. But I couldn't break up with Katje right away.
I loved her too much. To make it easier, I called her less and less
often. One day, when she complained about that, I told her it
was over. I couldn't eat much for several weeks.

– H. from Egypt

3   Illusion or reality

What do we imagine about each other's cultures?

The notion that "Frenchmen are romantic" is a *generalization* that is simply not always so. Thinking that Henri will bring flowers every day because he's French is called *stereotyping*. It may or may not be so! Such generalizations and stereotypes often lead to disappointments and surprises.

An educated man from an East African country wanted to marry a North European because, he thought, "all the women in my culture are more concerned with home affairs, and I would like a wife who can speak intelligently with me." But when he found and married an educated European, he discovered the downside to having an educated wife: She was career-bound and hardly had time or the energy to talk to him when she came home from work.

Stereotypes often exist below the consciousness. When they do, a partner might react without knowing why. Stereotypes can become a problem when one individual turns out to be quite different from the norm of his or her culture.

There are several ways to avoid stereotyping and generalizing:

- Get to know others from that same culture to compare and get a clearer picture of what is generally true of many, but not necessarily true of your partner.

- Read books or watch movies about your partner's culture and talk honestly about your observations and reactions.

- Visit the partner's country and family. If possible, live there for a few months. This may not be easy if you do not know or understand the language, but such a visit can provide some firsthand understanding of your partner's culture.

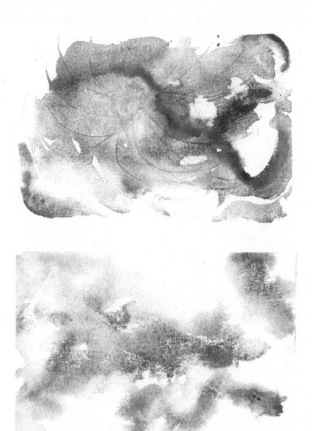

Blue and yellow make greens.

No two paintings are alike.

Water colors have a will of their own. The colors flow into one another in differing intensities and in different proportions. Different blues and different yellows will give a new feel. More blue and less yellow, or more yellow and less blue — the possibilities for multiple shades of green are endless.

But who chooses how much? Who decides? And how much water is needed to dilute the effect?

No two couples are the same!

- When you notice something in your partner's culture that is new or offensive to you, try to label it as "different," rather than "bad," and ask your partner about it.

- Find out the rationale and true reasons behind the practices you see that are different.

- Avoid generalizing. Instead of saying, "All Chinese do …" such and such, say, "Many or some Chinese do …" Remember that not everyone is the same, not even in one given culture.

- Keep a journal, using it to note the stereotypes you become aware of and how your partner does or might differ from them.

TO THINK AND TALK ABOUT (1)

Stereotypes

After you list your generalizations and stereotypes of your partner's culture, then ask your partner:

"Is this true of you? Is this true of your family? Is this mostly true of your culture, or country? How are you similar to your own people? How are you similar to my own?"

---

4 World citizens

Where do I belong?

Did you or your partner spend a significant part of your childhood or youth outside the parents' culture? Do you feel most at ease with others who have had a similar experience? If so, you or your partner would be called a **"third culture kid"** or **TCK** for short.

Through their bicultural or multicultural experience while growing up, TCK's have developed a unique ability to build relationships with people from other cultures, regardless of what those other cultures might be. They do not necessarily, or fully, identify with any of those cultures, yet they can borrow elements from each culture and assimilate them into their own life experience. Their sense of belonging is primarily in their relationship with others who share similar experiences rather than in a geographical place. They each truly belong only to one particular, unique world, and that world lies somewhere between the home or homes of the parents and the home where the TCK grew up.

The non-TCK partner can never truly understand that world, but he or she can learn to recognize and appreciate its impact on the relationship. Henneke, for instance, grew up in Malaysia where her Dutch father was working for a Dutch company. At home her family spoke Dutch, but at school she studied in the English language. Although the whole family visited Holland and their relatives twice a year, her understanding of the world was definitely more Asian than Dutch. She met and married a Dutch man who grew up in Holland and who had a definite attachment to Europe. It wasn't until their honeymoon in the Malaysian town where she had grown up that her husband realized how different her Dutch world was from his. That visit had a positive and lasting impact on his understanding of his bride.

What may seem to be even more complicated is a relationship between a TCK from one set of cultural backgrounds and a TCK from another combination of cultures. But this is not necessarily so. They may understand each other better than others because they respect what they don't understand. They are willing to ask questions and learn from each other, which makes it so much easier for them to resolve any conflicts and misunderstandings they might have.

If you and your partner are interested in learning more about those who have grown up with this mobile upbringing, you would benefit by reading *Third Culture Kids* by Pollock and Van Rekin. (See Further Reading List in Appendix III.)

5   Cross-signals of interest

How do we show that we like or love each other?

In a relationship, most people want to know how their partner feels about them — not just in the beginning, but even later as the relationship continues. This is done through signals — either in word, body language, or deed. In an intercultural, multicultural society, these signals often get misunderstood, or crossed.

A man in his twenties enters the post office with a load of packages in hand and stands behind a young woman in line. This woman makes eye contact with him briefly, and he with her, and she smiles. That eye contact and smile could mean many different things to many different people, and it may depend on where this scenario takes place. In the southern United

States, she might merely be polite and mean no more. It does not necessarily mean that the woman is ready to go to bed with the man; instead, she may merely feel sorry for him because he is carrying a load of packages, or she might merely be happy that *she* is not the one carrying a load of packages. Or, it could also be that she finds him curious or handsome and would like to start a conversation with him.

The safest way is never to assume anything. In the USA, an appropriate response for the man could be to smile back at her and say, "May I ask why you smiled at me just now?" Or he could look away and pretend he did not notice it.

Cross-signals of affection and of sexual attraction not only occur between two different cultures. They are also common within any culture where older traditional values conflict with those of the more modern (especially Western) ones. All these cross-signals result in many differing individual expectations.

For example, signs of flirting through eye contact (with whom and how long?), posture, words, and touch — all these differ from culture to culture. In some cultures, only prostitutes would look into a strange man's eyes in public, and if men from those cultures come to the West, they are often confused by women who do the same. In Spain and some Central American countries, it is common and acceptable for a man to follow closely behind a strange woman and to call out repeated compliments; but this might be considered harassment or even stalking, which is illegal in northern European and North American countries.

Never assume anything.
It is important to ask early on
what certain body language, facial expressions,
or eye contact of your partner may mean.

Dating and courting customs also differ from culture to culture, and in the West, from individual to individual. Using a friend to deliver the message that one person wants to date or get to know another is perhaps considered old-fashioned among northern Europeans, but it is still quite acceptable among others.

The expression of interest or of love while dating or even in marriage is not the same around the world. In some cultures, saying "I love you" to one's partner is uncommon and may even be unthinkable. A man would express his love and devotion by action, such as by providing for the family; and to him, that would be enough. But to a Western woman, or to a woman influenced

12

by Western movies, novels, or plays, such responsible behavior might not be enough. Likewise, sex and physical affection can be powerful communication signals, but even these might not be enough.

To feel loved and appreciated, one woman might like direct feelings and endearing words of flattery such as "You are beautiful" or "I love you very much" not just before sex, but at other times as well. Another woman would like to receive flower bouquets, expensive jewelry, tickets to a ball or concert, an exclusive restaurant dinner, or endearing e-mails or handwritten notes. A third might prefer a touch on the arm throughout the day, a massage, eye contact, nose rubbing, cheek strokes, a favorite song, or the gift of time in the form of a nature-walk while holding hands.

In a modern world where it would be wise not to take anything for granted, especially not the faithfulness or commitment of a partner, such continued romantic actions and words are important expressions of ongoing love and appreciation, long after a marriage commitment is made.

Do you know how your partner feels about *you*? How can you be sure? Does your partner know how *you* feel so that the right message gets across?

Expressions of feelings

Ask yourself which expressions of feelings of love or affection would you like to receive from your partner? Then compare your list with that of your partner:

- eye contact, smiling eyes, smiling mouth
- touch, massage, use of "pet names," being listened to
- music, gifts, praise, endearing words, love letters, poems
- being nearby, working at home
- cleaning, cooking for me, taking me out to eat or for a walk
- other ways?

Talk about which are hard for you to receive or do, and why.

6 Cross-signals of intentions and motives

What do we really want from our partner?

The attention is there. The chemistry is there. The feeling is there. Everything else seems so right. But could it be that one of the partners has hidden motives for the relationship? Maybe it's not love or marriage for love's sake at all. Perhaps, instead, it's all a show in order to gain a residential permit or visa. For example, a man's wish to stay in the country of a certain woman might be so great that he *thinks* he is attracted to her, when, in fact, this is not so at all.

The question is, what would happen to the relationship once this partner's ulterior goal is achieved? Would the relationship be as strong and promising if these motives or goals did not exist?

**If you are led to believe
that you are *the only* solution,
then you may end up being *only* a solution,
and no more.**

Anne, a British woman, met the sweet and charming Ali from Iran on the Internet. He said he was working for his brother in a city two hours from her house in England. Within six months, he married her. Her whole family turned up for the wedding. When he applied for residency, her father was asked to vouch for his character, even though the father didn't really know him. After they married, he continued to work for his brother two hours away and would only come home on weekends. One day he never came home at all.

HOT TIPS:

- Insist that the partner explore all other options for getting a work or residence visa before you give in to his or her pressure to marry.

- Be sure you understand the current laws of your country regarding a citizen of your country marrying a non-resident.

- Ask yourself: Once the residency permit is obtained, what will happen to the relationship? Would I really want to marry this person even if it were not for visa reasons? Or, would this person marry me if it were not for visa reasons? If so, how can I be sure?

---

7   Fling for now or cling forever

What if our situation changes?

Two artists visiting an art gallery discover that they share a passion for the same styles of art. However, once they work together in the art studio, they may discover they cannot *stand* each other! And so it is with two who fall in love.

Being in love — that feeling of "butterflies" in the stomach, the longing to be with a certain someone no matter what it costs, that attempt to overcome all barriers and the willingness to sacrifice all for the other — it does happen! When, how, and where love strikes becomes a set memory, and later even a trigger for the same feelings.

A couple who meet for the first time at a university laboratory will always cherish that place. The man who strikes up a conversation for the first time when helping a woman lift a box of heavy paper into the recycling bin may go back there for years on their anniversary just to have that special feeling again.

And then the situation between them changes. The university lab and the recycling bin will not be permanent parts of their environment. Two people who meet at sea will eventually live on land. Students eventually become career-bound. The adventure vacation ends when people return to their homes and the "daily grind." As circumstances, routines, and environments change,

15

that special feeling that began back then may eventually weaken and become a memory. Commitment or no commitment, wedding ceremony or not, the relationship itself may fade into an insignificant and feeling-less one. That in-love feeling might disappear, and with it, the sexual attraction and even the desire to be around that person.

When that happens, partners might feel they are in a sinking ship. Abandoning ship right away is not the only solution. In fact, to break an engagement or a marriage is considered shameful and devastating in some cultures. It would be much less painful and more sensitive to end the relationship *before* an engagement.

There are two other possibilities. Partners can stay true to each other, hoping that the in-love feeling will return (which it often does, at least from time to time). Or, they can work on deepening their friendship into one of loving, mutual care, and loyalty — even if that special feeling or even the sexual desire between them is not there anymore.

8 Trial and error

What about "trying it out to see if it works"?

Many couples think that before marrying, they should live together for a while to see if their relationship would work. While such trial partnerships occur and are even accepted in many Western countries, some studies in the past have shown that an intended trial partnership has a lesser chance of surviving than formally sealed partnerships. There are several reasons why:

- A "trial commitment" is an oxymoron — a phrase that contradicts itself. You cannot try out a flight on an airplane without flying one. You cannot even travel around the world in a flight simulator, although you may have the experience of seeming to fly. Likewise, living in with someone on a trial basis never gives the true picture.

- Severing a relationship is always painful and will leave scars, whether the relationship lasts only a few weeks or years. These scars will often impact or even prevent future relationships.

- Moving in with a partner with the intention of leaving him or her if things get "bumpy" cheapens or devalues you and/or your partner. It's fraud, just as is buying a coat and wearing it for a few days, then bringing it back to the store for a refund.

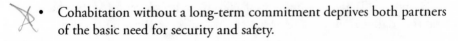

- Cohabitation without a long-term commitment deprives both partners of the basic need for security and safety.

- A commitment to growing old together "till death do us part" makes allowances for ups and downs, resulting in a more secure and relaxed atmosphere and a deeper intimacy.

- For centuries, many cultures and religious groups have been against such trial partnerships, and many of them still are. When individuals break away from the religion or tradition of their ancestors, they often "throw out the baby with the bathwater"; that is, they discard not only useless rules but also the really good ones which are healthy and preserve their society. As an example, apart from celibacy and total abstinence, monogamy (having only one sex partner for life) is still the best prevention from sexual diseases. (Of course, both partners must be committed to this!)

"The first twenty years we lived in your country; for the next twenty years let's live in mine."

9 Start-up, sync, and timing

Whose body belongs to whom and when?

When is sexual intimacy allowed? This is a question that varies from culture to culture and from individual to individual. For some, engagement is as sacred a vow as marriage, and therefore a sexual relationship is considered acceptable during the engagement period. In places where traditional wedding ceremonies are either too expensive for the family or impossible during a war, the sexual union and cohabitation of a period of time is viewed by that society as a common-law marriage and therefore permissible.

In Western countries, the rules vary quite a bit. Television and movies often give the impression (at least to those from non-western countries) that there are no moral standards or boundaries in the Western society. This is not true. Recent surveys indicate that over four out of five American families believe their children should refrain from a sexual union until *after* a marriage ceremony (whether religious, civil, or private family ceremony).[1] Even for whom "waiting" is not important, it is still socially unacceptable to "sleep around" or "cheat" on one's uncommitted partner.

Of course there are some who do not follow them, or those who have an entirely different set of rules, or none at all. The authors therefore advise people *never* to assume any action or intent by a partner or potential partner without talking about their specific rules and expectations.

Mary and George assumed too much. They met at a ball, danced together, and then went to her place to talk. They "hit it off" well in conversation and she laughed a lot. When he began to make sexual advances, she tried to stop him. All she had wanted was an opportunity to get to know him better, but he had assumed she wanted more. He became insistent, then forceful. She struggled away. "Why did you bother to invite me in?" he asked angrily, and left. The next morning, the police appeared at his door with a summons to appear in court. He was being charged with sexual assault.

The events above are not only an obvious case of cross-signals, but also one of a violation of boundaries. When Mary first began to say "No," George did not take her seriously. He did not know that even in Western cultures moral behavior and expectations can be quite different from the "norms," such as portrayed in American and European movies.

Whenever one partner expresses his or her boundaries with a "No, not yet" or "Not now," it is simply safer and more loving of the other to comply. In Western and many other countries, it is also the *law* to do so.

To prevent any future misunderstanding or embarrassment, the questions George needs to consider are:

- Do I know the rules of the land I live in pertaining to sexual behavior?

- Do I know this girl's religious, social, or personal boundaries?

- How do I respond when a girl says, "No" or "Stop"? Can I talk with her about her reasons without forcing her to give what I want?

---

[1] The Zogby poll was completed in April of 2007 and can be found on-line at http://www. abstinenceassociation.org/docs/zogby_questionnaire_050207.pdf

And the questions Mary needs to think about are:

- What signals might I give that sends the wrong message about what I do or don't want?

- What signals might my partner show that he expects to have more of me sexually?

- How and when can I tell him that I am not or not yet interested or ready?

- If my partner does not respect my boundaries, such as "Not now," what should I do about it?

Many young people today are discovering that it is wiser to get to know a person first, talk about their personal history, their ideals or their views on relationship or sex before they enter into a more "serious" romantic and/or sexual relationship. Young men still prefer to marry a woman with a good reputation, meaning someone who has not "slept around" with other men.

The authors agree with those psychologists and medical authorities who believe that sex within a monogamous relationship is much, much safer than it is when practiced with several different partners. Even today, despite the so-called "safe sex" methods available, "serial monogamous"[2] behavior is anything but safe. Most birth control products do nothing to prevent diseases from spreading; not even condoms are 100% effective. This is why many young people claim that sex is more satisfying (and relaxing!) when they are able to trust each other's faithfulness and devotion.

Could it be, then, that the old laws of morality were right, after all? Or that they were not intended to "spoil our fun," but simply intended to protect us as individuals and as a society?

TO THINK AND TALK ABOUT (3)

Boundaries of Sexual Expression

What are the rules of my family, society, religious leaders and the laws of my country in regards to sexual behavior before marriage?
During marriage?

---

[2] *Polygamy* is where one person has multiple spouses or multiple *concurrent* partners. *Serial monogamy* is characterized by two or more *consecutive*, monogamous relationships.

How are these rules different from those of my partner's parents, country or society?
How are they different in the country where I presently live?
How are they different in the country where we plan to live?
What are my boundaries? Yours?

---

10 Back up support

Will our parents support this relationship?
What if not?

When members of one of the partner's family reject or even mistreat the partner that is different, it leads to a feeling of "I don't belong to them," and it really hurts! The reasons for this rejection include differences in race, ethnic background, religion, class, status, language, dialect, accent, level of education, career, personality, age, or level of wealth. The questions will then be:

- Will the partner be able to cope with the family's rejection and mistreatment? How will the rejected partner respond?

- How will this rejection affect the relationship between the partners?

 • Where else will the couple find emotional support?

If one set of parents is against a couple's partnership or marriage from the beginning, anything could be expected — from cold, distant tolerance to outright, nasty hostility. Racial and ethnic prejudice of parents can be so deep-seated that no matter how well the "different" partner adjusts to their culture or expectations, they might still disapprove. And this, of course, can put a great strain on that partner, the couple, and the whole family. One father from a non-Western nation offered $10,000 to his American daughter-in-law as a bribe to divorce his son and return to her country. Out of fear, she took the money and left. The family destroyed the son's passport and documents, and it took many months before he was able to replace it and return to his wife in America.

An earlier, open conversation with one's parents about what they want or don't want in their son- or daughter-in-law might prevent such pain. To a Western mind it seems unreasonable for parents or family members to pretend to give their child the freedom to decide, bravely swallow their disappointment in their child's decision until after the wedding, and then to make life miserable for the son- or daughter-in-law thereafter.

One long-term effect of parental disapproval is that the parents often speak badly about their daughter- or son-in-law in front of the grandchildren. Because these grandchildren are caught in the middle, they suffer the most. The strain and tensions that result have no end, even long after the divorce, in case that should occur.

Here are some tips for preventing future trouble:

- If you have met someone whom you are considering partnering with for life, introduce that special someone to your family early on in the relationship and ask the family members for their honest reaction. Their opinion will be an indicator as to how they might respond to this person in the future.

- If you are the potential partner yourself, try your best to develop a good relationship with your partner's family before you commit to marrying, and especially before you have children.

- If you sense that family members of your partner do not accept you, or their disapproval and distrust seem to grow instead of diminish, you have several options: (1) talk with your partner about your desire to keep a healthy distance from them; (2) reconsider a future commitment to that partner; or (3) explore ways you can stay with your partner and still win the hearts of your in-laws.

If you choose the third one, it might take years of creative exploration before that in-law thinks and feels differently toward you. But it can pay off! One wise woman said it this way, "Always look for ways to show kindness to your mother-in-law. It is the key to your husband's heart. However much a woman would like her man to be just her husband, he will always be a son."

If your partner seems to be constantly caught in the middle between his family and you, it may appear that he cannot decide who is more important — the family or you. This is not necessarily so. It may be that his cultural ethics require him to respect his parents, and that such respect includes never to speak out against them or to disregard their wishes.

Family acceptance

Do my parents accept my partner?
Do my siblings, grandparents, cousins, etc. accept my partner?
Does my community or society accept my partner?
If the answer is "no" to the above, how does my partner react?
Do his or her parents accept me?
If not, how do they behave? How do I react?
Do the siblings, grandparents, cousins, etc. accept me?
If not, how do they show it? How do I react?
Will they (or do they) accept our children?
What do I value / dislike about both of our families?
How can I personally help to foster their acceptance?

11 Words and hand signals

Do we understand what we say to each other?

Working on this art project are two partners who are very different from each other. This is why, if the art project is to turn out well, the two artists would have to talk a lot together before they can *do* anything together.

Similarly, intercultural partners who want to make their partnership a satisfying one must take the time to collaborate, that is, to talk and negotiate together. They must agree as to where they will live and work, which identity and culture they will adapt to, how many children they will have, and many other considerations (see Chapters 3 and 4).

But how would they do that if they don't fully understand each other's language? Misunderstandings happen even among partners who speak the same language. Even more such misunderstandings will occur between partners whose language-of-origin differs.

Communication is made up of various aspects. All of the following vary from culture to culture.

Language. This, first of all, is the most obvious aspect. It has been said that one's heart language, or one's first language, speaks volumes that can never be expressed in the second or third language. Even the personality, the voice, and the thought processes can vary when one changes languages. Learning the language of the partner is not always easy. For example, 60% of the English language is made up of idioms (a group of words that denote one meaning). In many of the Chinese and Indochinese languages, the tone or inflexion is more important than a word itself and can completely affect its meaning.

Direct vs. Indirect. These styles of communication characterize how and to whom one communicates a message. The *direct* style is clear and to the point and directly spoken to the person for whom the message is intended. For example, "I'm sorry, I can't come," is direct, as opposed to the indirect style, "I will do my best to come to your party and will let you know later," when in fact, the speaker knows that acceptance would never be possible. The *indirect* style may involve stories, more words, flattery, metaphors, questions, and rather vague messages — to the western mind at least. Sometimes these messages may be communicated through a third person, such as sending your friend or spouse in your place and asking him or her to tell the hostess you were unable to come.

Linear vs. Circular. These are styles used when people make their point or answer a question. Linear communication is like a straight line: The main point is made first; then related sub points are selected and added. Circular communication discusses around the heart of the matter and emphasizes the context (surrounding information) rather than the main point itself.

Nonverbal or emotional expression is an even more significant part of communication. Posture, hand and foot gestures, eye movements, facial expression, the volume and tone of voice — all have a language of their own which vary from culture to culture. It takes years to learn the many variations and their uniqueness. Every culture, subculture, and family has its own rules and habits when expressing emotions such as anger, joy, humor, frustration, love, pride, endearment, impatience, contentment, discontentment, attachment, loneliness, stress, insecurity, anxiety, and fears. For example, how do you feel when your friend shouts at you in an angry tone when you are late? Or laughs out loud in public when you say something your partner perceives as funny? Or smiles broadly when nervous? In some cultures it is acceptable to shout when angry and to restrain any outward sign of sadness. In others, it is the opposite.

There are varieties of learned behavior. It is therefore not so easy to judge someone to be abnormal, impolite, or unstable until you first understand the norms of his or her culture. Also, persons from two cultures might have a totally different way of showing how they feel about themselves in relation to each other. Because they also have various interpretations of each other's words, body language, and behaviors, these can easily be misunderstood or judged incorrectly.

People from most Asian and Arab cultures and other collective cultures tend to place more importance on nonverbal and implicit communication. In some of these cultures it is expected that you keep silent when you disagree with your partner, because to speak might bring shame upon yourself or your partner. In contrast, people from North America and northern Europe tend to value verbal communication more highly when sending and receiving messages. They value honesty and truth above honor and respect. (To learn more about this, refer to Sarah Lanier's book, *Foreign to Familiar*. See Further Reading List in Appendix III.)

TO THINK AND TALK ABOUT (5)

Communication styles

Observe your families and each other's families. Which of the following behaviors are commonly practiced in your and your partner's families?

Direct–Verbal

Verbal expression of wants or needs; tone, choice of words

Use of actual name or terms of endearment

Honest and direct expressions of feelings, ideas, thoughts

Flattery, compliments, praise

Strong language: curse words, or abuse of sexual terms, name calling

Refusal or disagreement (how?)

Linear, to the point

Brief, simple

Indirect–(Verbal or non-verbal)

Silence; use of pauses

Gestures with hands, fingers, body posture

Frown, tears, mouth curved downward

Head shaking, hanging, nodding side-ways, up and down

Tone of voice (expressing emotions)

Soft voice, loud voice

Sarcasm; teasing (either as indirect anger or as endearment)

Other styles

Monologue: speaking without waiting for response

Dialogue: speaking briefly and expecting a response

Interrupting or overlapping

Flowery language: hyperboles and exaggerations

Defensive, argumentative for sake of control

Circular, emphasis on context

Tell each other what you like about each other's style of communication. Then talk about what you wish the other would do differently.

---

12 Maturity

Am I mature enough to function as a partner?

Many people blame their relationship problems on personality differences. Some blame them on their cultural differences. While these differences can be very challenging, they can be an opportunity for partners, or potential partners, to ask themselves, "What needs to change, or mature *in me,* so that I can better handle those differences?"

A pair of three-year olds can hardly be expected to work well on a challenging art project together, can they? Three-year olds don't share or compromise easily, they don't know how to negotiate, and they haven't learned to consider the needs of others or to accept each other's unique skills. Rather, they will use violence or throw a temper tantrum to get what they want, and they might even destroy each other's contribution to their work of art! Most people would call such behavior *immature* or *childish*.

As people get older, they normally become more mature. But unfortunately not all become mature enough to make a relationship work, especially if it is an intercultural one. In fact, many partners who separate after a given time can trace their problems to the immaturity or childishness of at least one of them.

The more mature a person,
the better a partner he or she will be,
especially in an intercultural relationship.
But what does it mean to be mature?

To some, maturity might mean having enough money and a house, or being independent financially, or having a set career and a steady income. In some cultures, a woman is considered mature when she is able to give birth to a child, perhaps at age 13; in other cultures, a boy becomes of age at 12. In the West, people are thought to be mature when they are able to …

- separate feelings from reason,
- be responsible for themselves within the cultural, ethical, and legal boundaries of the society in which they live,
- ask (not demand) someone to fulfill their needs or wants,
- consider possible future consequences of their actions,
- accept the reality of both their own strengths and limitations,
- be open to the correction and advice of others,
- acknowledge the strengths and abilities of others,
- accept the reality of other people's limitations and failures,
- be aware of the needs of others,
- act out of compassion, not out of a personal need to be loved,
- forgive (not seek revenge), yet protect themselves,
- be loyal and honest in relationships,
- react with culturally acceptable self-control when agitated,

- deal with stress and anger without hurting others,
- carry out expected responsibilities within the family,
- actively seek stability financially, socially, and emotionally,
- willfully and appropriately accept or reject the beliefs, preferences, emotional reactions, and behaviors of others,
- know when to confront and when to maintain peace.

The second question to ask is, if I'm not mature enough, how can I become more mature?

If you think you are still far from mature, there is no need to panic. The important thing is that you work on getting there. Maturity is a relative term. The more mature you are, the more capable you are in handling challenging life situations. Conversely, the more life situations you experience, the more mature you will get. This process continues all during life. It is furthered by listening to and observing others, by reading books, by interacting with others, and by learning from mistakes.

Becoming mature is a process.
You will never achieve perfect maturity
but you can make it your goal!

One indication that you might be mature enough to handle a relationship with someone from another culture, and to do so well, is that you can laugh at yourself and enjoy the present. Another indication is that you are open to adopting new roles, behaviors, and perspectives. Perhaps asking others to point out some areas you have yet to mature in is a sign of maturity as well! Ask them, "Do you think I can handle a long-term commitment without ruining or hurting the other person?" might be risky. But if they say "no," you could ask them for some tips on areas you have yet to grow in.

13 True love

Am I mature enough to love well?

The best sign of maturity is to be able to love well. This is not to be confused with the wonderful feeling of being *in love* or being sexually attracted to someone. Nor is it the same as the flattery of knowing that someone is attracted to you. These feelings are all wonderful, but will they alone be powerful enough to keep you and your partner happy together for the rest of your lives?

Transparent honesty

Perhaps you can see the translucent half of the seed pods from the plant, Honesty. The seeds develop between two fragile, silky-to-touch, wafer-thin films. The outer filament that holds the two sides together is delicate but strong — until the seeds are released.

In this collage, these seed pod halves are layered with other transparent or translucent papers. If you look closely, you will see that the large leaf at the back lets the sunlight through except where dark shadows are cast by other leaves.

Transparency, or honesty, serves an important function in relationships. Should dishonesty get in the way at any level, it throws shadows over openness.

**Unless people expose their innermost being
and share their thoughts and feelings,
the "seeds of truth" can never bear "fruit."**

In the Greek language there are several different words for love. The feeling of emotional and sexual attraction is called *eros*. Not all men are attracted to the same woman, and not all women are attracted to the same man. In many Western relationships, this kind of love seems to be *the only* basis for marriage. When the feeling ends, the relationship ends. This view explains why so many marriages in the Western world, and increasingly elsewhere, fail. These partners think that when they feel nothing anymore, or if they begin to get tired or get angry with each other, it is time to look for another partner.

Then there is *phileo* or brotherly love within family members and close friends. This is sometimes a feeling and sometimes an action-oriented love. It assumes trust, sometimes commitment, comradeship, friendliness, and care. It is also an important and growing aspect of a long-lasting relationship between two married partners. It involves loyalty during sickness and trials. It might also be expressed in joyfully giving gifts.

Yet another word for love in the Greek language is *agape* — the kind of love that sacrifices unconditionally. Even more powerful than *eros* and *phileo*, it will hold you together even when there are occasional disappointments, hurts, and cause for anger. It outlasts both that initial feeling of *eros* and the status of *phileo*. This *agape* love is described by St. Paul in the Bible as follows:

> *Love (agape) is patient, love is kind. It does not envy, it does not boast, it is not proud. It is not rude, it is not self-seeking, it is not easily angered, it keeps no record of wrongs. Love does not delight in evil but rejoices with the truth. It always protects, always trusts, always hopes, always perseveres. Love never fails.*
> *— 1st Corinthians 13: 4-8, the Bible*

Agape love is not a warm, mushy feeling, but a choice and action. It is based on the belief that you and I are fallible but valuable, and that you and I are of equal worth. This belief makes us willing to sacrifice for another even when the other person disappoints us.

This kind of love involves receiving that person into the family for life and committing time, money, and resources to the welfare of that person for the rest of his or her life. It is similar to adoption. The initial feeling of *eros* might have long disappeared and the familial *phileo* might be taken for granted, but when there is *agape* love, something far more powerful becomes available: and that is *grace,* that is, undeserved forgiveness. (See more about forgiveness in Chapter 5).

Please note: Only if your sacrifice helps the partner *in the long run* is it a sign of true love. While this kind of love respects and views the other person as valuable, it does not have to accept everything that other person says or does. Both your *phileo* and *agape* love make that other person's *ultimate welfare* your priority. That could mean that if your partner is involved in an addiction that is harmful to his wellbeing (such as a compulsive gambling, alcohol abuse, or drug dependency), it would not at all be a sign of love if you constantly came to the rescue. The more loving thing to do would be to let this partner pay for the consequences of his own behavior, not out of revenge, but to help him recognize his need to change and/or to seek professional help.

TO THINK AND TALK ABOUT (6)

Maturity

Am I becoming increasingly able to …

- consciously accept or reject the beliefs, preferences, and behaviors of persons in my upbringing?

- respect other people's ways of seeing and doing things?

- be open to the advice and perspective of others?

- respond to the needs of others, not out of a need to be loved, but simply for the ultimate welfare of others?

- forgive the wrong of others, yet find measures to protect myself from repeated injustice?

- be honest in the relationship that is important to me?

- be loyal and committed even when it isn't easy?

- carry out expected responsibilities?

- be willing to lay aside some preferences, yet find ways to keep my own unique identity?

- maintain a sense of humor and enjoy the present?

In my culture, what qualities would be found in a mature person? Am I considered mature enough to partner with someone who is culturally different? Is my partner?

Chapter 2 Settling on a Studio location

Where will we partner together?

The light — its source, direction, intensity and color — has a profound effect on how the artist envisions the development of his or her final work. An artist who grew up and works under the strong, intense light of Cyprus expresses his art quite differently from an artist who grew up and paints pictures in the relatively dull light of England. Imagine if the artist in Cyprus would begin the piece of art in Cyprus, then pass it on to the artist in England to complete it! That would be unthinkable. If they want to produce an artwork together, they had better first decide where that work will take place.

The partner who grew up in one culture might see and interpret the world quite differently than the one who grew up in another culture. The physical aspect of an area where a person grows up also influences people differently. For example, people who have grown up in the mountains have a different feeling of the sky than those who have grown up on the plains. People who have grown up in a country surrounded by water feel as though they have an unlimited horizon. Those born and raised in a landlocked country feel more connected to the people who live beyond their country's boundaries than those who have oceans between them. Those who have grown up on an island could have the same sense of isolation as those who live in a village surrounded by mountains or in the middle of a desert. Each group is impacted differently by the sound of crashing waves, the sight of falling snow, and the sting of a driving sandstorm.

This variation of experiences is true not only of art partners, but also of marriage or relationship partners. Partners who grow up in one culture and move to another often experience quite a shock and an enormous loss. Their earlier experience will affect the way they see and experience not only the new physical environment, but also the social context in which the couple now live. The workplace, the language, the people, and the school and playground of the children-all will seem different because they *are* different.

Furthermore, when there is a change of countries for one of the partners, the balance in the relationship changes for both. The woman who is in her culture will feel naturally more in control and self-assured than her husband who is new to that culture. She might at first be a leader in some areas where he knows less or is less experienced. This will of course reverse if the couple should move to his country.

There are six options to consider:

- Staying in the country where the partners met

- Moving to the partner's country

- Moving back to the home country

- Taking turns

- Straddling both countries: his and hers

- Moving into a neutral country

Because all of the above options depend on visa restrictions and citizenship rights and the like, this chapter ends with a brief look at issues related to the laws of the land.

1   Staying where the partners met

Let's say an international student from India meets an Austrian woman in Vienna; they marry and continue to live in Austria. According to the immigration laws at the time of this writing, once his student visa ends, he is required to return to India in order to wait several months for a residential visa. In other countries, this process might even take longer.

There are many advantages to staying in the country where the couple met. The cultural environment of the country where the couple met is the same as the one where they decide to live in the future. There are fewer surprises, and perhaps even less stress. Of course, this all depends partly on how well the "foreign" partner has already adjusted to his or her new environment, and how well both partners understand each other's cultures.

"Eating dinner with you is one custom I will never change when I go back to my country."

To consider:

- The real motive of the foreign partner to marry a citizen of the desired country might not be love or a life commitment, but a faster way to obtain a permanent visa. The question the citizen needs to ask his or her partner is, "Will you stay with me even after you get your permanent visa?" There is no telling how honest an answer the partner will give.

- The questions the foreign partner needs to ask early on is this: "If I would not get a permanent visa even after I married, would I still want to marry this person? Would this person want to come back to my country? Could he or she?"

- One partner might not always interpret the behavior of the other correctly until both have spent some time in each other's country. It would therefore be wise if each partner spends at least two months in each other's homeland, if possible, before the partners make a long-term commitment to each other.

A North African woman met and married an Algerian who had been brought up in France and was a French citizen. Their children grew up speaking French and went to local French schools. Sadly, her husband died. The question she had not asked until that point was: "As a non-citizen, do I have the right to remain in France with my French children who are too young to live on their own?"

33

2 Moving to the partner's country

Before Jay left his country, he thought he would want to stay with Helena forever and pictured Greece to be like paradise on earth. But soon after he arrived, he discovered that since there were so many different ways of doing things, it would take years to learn them all. He not only needed to learn the language and adjust to the different customs, food, music, rules and regulations, and so on. He also struggled to feel accepted by the family and by the community. In summary, he was experiencing **culture shock**.

When he had met Helena in Canada three years earlier, he had been fascinated by her beautiful dark eyebrows and long hair, her charm, her taste in clothes. But now that she was among her own people, she seemed to have lost some of her uniqueness. Besides, she showed signs of getting tired of teaching him and explaining things to him, and she smiled less.

When Jay finally landed a job, he was surprised to find that his fellow workers, his boss, and many of the other dynamics associated with the work place were different from what he was accustomed to. The more relaxed attitude at work and fewer work hours suited him less than expected. He was used to a different structure and to earning more money.

Soon he felt as though he simply didn't belong there at all. He missed his favorite food, his friends and relatives, the cooler weather all year around, and the snowy mountains. He found it tiresome to learn the language, and he missed watching the sports channels in English. Eventually, he stopped asking Helena questions about the language and culture; because he could tell that she was tired of answering them.

When they began to argue about things that had never bothered either of them before, Helena began to realize what was happening. She remembered her own feelings of loss and frustration in her first year in Jay's country.

Jay might have prevented much of his pain had he visited Greece for a few months *before* he married and decided to live there. He might have been better prepared by assessing whether or not he would *want* to adjust to this new environment, culture, friends, and extended family, and by assessing what parts he could learn to accept. The visit would have also helped him to understand and appreciate Helena better.

If you should think of marrying someone from another country and eventually living there, you might consider the following:

- When you visit your partner's country before you decide to marry her and live there, ask yourself, "Can I lose my strong cultural traits without losing myself? Can I live with that culture long-term?"

- When you are there, you will at first be excited as you discover new things and meet all the family and friends. After that, it can be hard work and you might get tired. After a few months you might experience homesickness, that longing for your family, home, and culture which you left behind. This feeling will come and go even when everything else is going well for you in the new environment.

- Making friends with people who speak your language might help, as long as they encourage you to adapt and not only sympathize with you, and as long as you don't neglect to give your family the attention they need.

- Members of your partner's family might treat you differently after you get married or decide to stay there. The family rules and their expectations of you might turn out to be different than you expected.

- Your partner might be in reverse culture shock once you both move back to his or her home country (see section 3 "Moving back to the home country").

A few other considerations....

(a) Acceptance into the family

When Juan from Costa Rica first came to northeastern USA, he was treated rather coldly. It was as if the people there suspected him of being an alien from outer space. They were polite, but he felt no warmth from them, only mistrust. It took a long time before he felt he was "one of them" — in fact, a very long time, and certainly not in the way he had expected. He felt isolated and lonely, except when he was in the company of his own countrymen.

But it was the opposite for his American wife when she came to Juan's family clan years earlier. She was not accustomed to so much positive attention from strangers, such as a kiss on the cheek, their smiles, their curiosity and questions. She interpreted this to be a "nice show" of politeness. When this never really changed, she realized that their show of affection was genuine. At the same time she began to feel overwhelmed, and she longed for times to be on her own.

(b) Extended family expectations

Whichever way partners find each other, the expectations of the families might differ. In many parts of the world, it is expected that a wife must fit in, that is, to adjust to the extended family and society of her husband. For a woman from an individualistic society (usually Western) who marries someone from a collective culture, this would not be easy. Her husband's family members expect her to "fit in" — that is, to do what they say and want and to be involved in their family life. After all, she has now become part of them. However, if she is an individualist, she could find it difficult to get accustomed to her loss of freedoms and independence.

A woman from a collective society (such as in Asian or African countries) might feel unnecessary, not needed, nor wanted if her more individualistic, North European partner never tells her what to do. Another might feel used or belittled if he *does* tell her what to do! Both these women could feel lonely and abandoned. If either of them is unable to express her feelings, wants, or things that truly bother her, her individualistic partner would never know or understand.

What is normal to you could seem weird to others! A collective family might view the new partner as backward when he or she makes independent decisions. The individualistic partner, on the other hand, might judge the collective partner as emotionally dependent or immature. If only both could learn to view each other as culturally different, rather than as flawed or weak!

Special long-distance rates on the telephone or an Internet calling system can make affordable the many needed conversations. The acquaintance of an older, wiser parent-figure from within the new community could provide an additional source of emotional support.

> *John hated it when I was on the phone with my mom or my sister for an hour at a time. He felt left out, but mostly jealous, I think. He didn't have a close relationship with his brother, and his parents were dead. I tried to explain, but nothing helped. I finally decided to make those calls when he wasn't around. And when they called during dinner, I would let the voice mail answer and call back later.*
>
> *– Miriam*

3 Moving back to the home country

Moving back home sounds like a dream come true at last, but it can be quite a shock to return there. So many things have changed; other things are simply not remembered. The people are not the same: some have grown old, others have moved, and still others do not remember the returnee. New buildings have been built and landmarks have been torn down. Even the music has changed. The partner who is going back to his or her own country is in **reverse culture shock**.

Let's look at this from the point of view of Helena from Greece, who had studied in Canada and has returned home to Greece. Although she had really looked forward to coming home, she felt at first that she didn't really belong there anymore. Even worse, she felt totally estranged. Some things had changed while she was gone; there were new streets and many new houses. Some of her favorite landmarks were torn down. Even the music had changed on the radio. Some things were not as she would have liked them to be. Commodity products easily bought in Canada had not yet reached Greece. Instead, she had to get accustomed again to products that had not ever come to Canada. She was surprised to find that it is more difficult to re-adjust to her original home, plus its changes, than it was for her to adjust to Canada three years before. To her surprise, she missed Canada. She was experiencing reverse culture shock.

Another surprise was that being with the family again and in the old home environment re-awakened some of the old traits and practices she had abandoned while living in a foreign country. The interactions she observed again, the well-meaning pressure of her parents to conform to their customs again, and the traditions all around her brought out the old Helena that she was before and had left behind. Now they were all back, at least for now.

For her Canadian-born partner Jay, who was new to that culture, moving to Greece meant "culture shock" (see previous section). Worst of all, he couldn't understand at all what Helena was going through in her "reverse culture shock." He expected her to know everything and be there for him. But because she was still trying to re-adjust, she struggled to be patient with Jay. She tried at first, but soon she tired of helping him to learn the language and to adjust to the Greek culture. As she recovered from her reverse culture shock, she was able to help him in his adjustment.

To consider:

- Be patient. Reverse culture shock is even harder to recover from than the culture shock experienced during the first few months in a foreign country. You might also feel a sense of loss as you leave behind the culture or country you have worked so hard to adjust to.

- The presence and pressure of the family and the environment will re-awaken some of your old traits and practices. This could confuse your partner and create tensions between you. Give your partner time to adjust to this older version of who you are.

- Try to anticipate the shock and adjustment difficulties that your partner might have (see last section) by remembering what it was like for you when you were adjusting to his country.

- Listen to each other without judging or criticizing the other.

- Talk with your partner about your observations without making fun of him or her. Encourage each other; try to see the humorous and adventurous side of it all.

4   Taking turns

"When you marry someone from another country, be prepared for change!" commended Ann's mother when Ann fell in love with an Australian. "In a few years he'll want to move back to his country and take you with him. You'll see ..."

"True, Mother dear, but if he really does manage to take me there with him, I'll bring him back here again later!"

> *Before we were engaged to be married, I told my fiancé, "I plan to return to live in my country some day. But I don't think you'd want to go with me, would you?" To which he replied, "I'll consider that." And 30 years later he considered it, and moved to Austria with me. Eight years have gone by, and we still live there. He enjoys the trams, the fresh bread from the bakery, and the people on the street. He's even learned some German. But he misses all the American sports on TV, and that's a huge sacrifice for him. This year we're planning to move back to the USA again. I don't really want to, but it would only be fair. I think he's done enough to prove his love for me.*
> *— E. from Austria*

"Home is a country where fewer things need to be endured and more things can be enjoyed," said one refugee from a war-torn country. "And what I enjoy here is my wife and six children!" But years later, when peace was restored in his country, he moved back with his "foreign" wife and children.

Some day a partner might regret her promise, "I will follow you wherever you go." She might want or need to move back to her country later on and take him with her. A partner's well-intentioned promise of regular visits to the other's home country might need to be broken because of war, local family responsibilities, or changes in the family's financial situation.

One drawback of moving from one country to another, and back again, or somewhere else, is a lack of continuity of relationships with the extended family and friends. Each time a family moves, there is a repetition of the *tear and readjustment* phase. "Where do we belong?" is the question both parents and their children might ask.

5   Straddling two countries

The couple has two homes. They live in Spain in the winter and in England in the summer. Or, they run two or more hotel businesses that thrive in different places in different seasons. Straddling two or more countries is for people such as the rich, the very self-confident and secure, the ones who can perhaps afford two homes, the ones who can adjust easily or who love to travel, for those who don't mind separation now and then, or for those with an international business or a diplomatic job.

Many of the points mentioned in the other where-to-live options apply here. The significant difference is the constant change, the feeling of not really belonging deeply to one place but belonging to both.

This lifestyle can be both a challenge and a benefit to the children. (See section about "third culture kids" in Chapter 1, Section 4) They will grow up bi-culturally or multi-culturally, and their lives will be full of changes. They will benefit if they become fluent in the language of the countries in which they live, plus in the language of their parents. However, they might not become equally fluent in all these languages and therefore might need extra help with the language in which they will further their formal education. A bilingual school, a boarding school, or home tutoring would help meet that need. The need is particularly strong if the young person wants to return to their passport country to work or to study.

6   Moving to a neutral country

Many couples find that moving to or staying in a third culture works best for them because neither has a cultural advantage over the other. Reasons for this choice are varied. There is simply a desire to start afresh because of one of the following reasons: Opportunities are advantageous in the new country; one partner might be prevented from entering the country of the spouse; or, neither partner can return to his or her own home.

However, this is not always easy, especially if neither has lived there before. The following will need to be considered:

- Do your homework thoroughly before leaving. What was suggested in previous sections applies here for both partners. Valuable resources to prepare for the family move include: a prior visit to that country, the acquaintance of others who live there or have lived there, books about that country, travel guides and tourist information.

Insider or outsider

Where is this girl? Is she looking from the outside in through the glass? Can she see in? Is she looking from the inside out? Is she the guest or the hostess? Will she receive her guests graciously? Is she afraid of them? Will she be received graciously? Can she feel at home? Either way, her response is up to her.

If you were to answer these questions, where does your answer place you — on the inside or on the outside?

**In an intercultural relationship,
wherever the couple chooses to live,
at least one partner will be "on the outside"
in some way or other, and that's OK.**

- Each partner will adapt differently. Your partner might accept and even love one aspect of that culture, while you hate and reject it. One learns the language faster than the other. Various aspects of each new location will surprise each partner differently. The one who adjusts more quickly might not be willing to support the other partner who is slower to adjust. All this could seem like an exciting adventure, or it could lead to conflicts, tensions, misunderstandings, anger, confusion, disappointments, and constant re-negotiation.

- Family ties will be weakened. Help is not at hand as it might have been in one of the partner's home countries.

- Children might become multilingual, speaking and understanding other than their parents' languages. In most cases, a long-term stay in this country will mean that the child's main language will be the one used at school.

- Long-term issues must be faced. The first question is whether this option is to be permanent or temporary. If temporary, whose country will the couple go back to? Other aspects include: visa problems, adjustment on both sides, visits to both families of origin, the question of retirement and burial. For instance, a family in Cairo heard of the death of their grown daughter, who had journeyed away several years before to study and work in England. The deceased daughter's husband and most of her friends lived in the London area. The question posed to her Egyptian family was whether their daughter would be buried nearer to them in Cairo, or nearer to her own family in England.

> *No matter how hard we tried to ignore it, I found that one of us was always the outsider. This "outsider" feeling lessened the longer we were together, at least for me. Yet I sensed that at the same time while I was an outsider, I was also an insider. It was very confusing for me. Nothing was completely clear. Only when my husband experienced being an outsider himself did he understand how I felt.*
>
> *– A. from Finland*

TO THINK AND TALK ABOUT (7)

Choosing where to live — your country or mine?

The foreign partner should ask the other...

- If I should move back to my country some day, would you want to move there with me? Why or why not?

- How would our relationship change or develop?

- What would you like? What would you miss?

- Would you mind being taught by me? (Language, customs, rules) Would you be allowed to work there, considering visa regulations, the degree of education, career/job experience and training?

- Would my country be good for our children? Why or why not, and in what respects?

- Is there another country where we could both live?

- Where will you want to retire — in your country or in mine or in — ?

- Is it possible for you to become a citizen of my country?

If you met in a third country, ask each other these questions.

No one knows what will happen in the future. Circumstances, goals, opportunities, and desires change over the years. The cliché, "home is where the heart is" sounds very sweet, but it isn't that simple. Whatever country a couple should live in, there will always be things in that culture that one or both don't like. If they can endure what is difficult and find things they can both enjoy, that country can become home.

7 Learning the laws of the land

In whichever country a couple chooses to set up as home, it will never be just a place to live, but a place in which both residents are subject to the same laws. This is true regardless of whether one or both are citizens of that country.

As laws and ethics vary from country to country, and from state to state in certain other countries, it is important to get acquainted with the laws of the land you both choose to live in. Whether they be immigration laws, traffic regulations, marriage laws, or other social laws, these laws affect nearly every aspect of your life.

This is especially true of immigration laws. Limited and restrictive employment opportunities and non-accepted qualifications could narrow down some of the options. Finding a solution might take time, creativity, and lots of "leg work" for one or both partners.

Special attention should be given to those laws or rules (civil or religious) that protect the safety and well-being of each partner and the entire family. These laws differ from country to country; therefore both partners need to be aware of these differences. For example, in many countries it is illegal and punishable for one spouse to beat another, or for parents to physically punish their children; while in others, both these behaviors are considered a natural part of family life.

> *My husband said he will send me back to my country if I tell anyone how my face got bruised. I was scared, because he has all the papers for immigration, and I didn't want to go back to my country alone. My parents and family would ask many questions, and I would feel such shame. But now I know the law and my rights. The social agency is helping me so that I won't be sent back to my country. When my husband found out about this, he got scared and stopped beating me.*
>
> *-M. from the Philippines*

Not all such stories end this well. True, in many countries, immigration authorities will protect the battered wife from an unwanted deportation. Usually, men who have been violent once have an emotional weakness that causes them to be violent again, and that can sometimes be fatal for their physically weaker female partner. It would therefore be wiser for the victim to seek shelter and protection early on, to insist that the abuser gets professional help, to consider long-term separation until he does, and to divorce if he refuses to.

Laws concerning public or private behavior between the sexes also vary from country to country. For example, what is an accepted pursuit of a woman by a man in one country might be labeled as sexual harassment in another. Sexual assault (attempting to force one's partner to have sexual relations even after that partner refuses) is punishable by law in many countries.

A note about children: In countries where religious authority and political government are intertwined, the couple should definitely be informed about how religious law would affect the children's freedom to choose, their right to inherit, as well as their custody in case of parental divorce.

The most important points to keep in mind are as follows:

- The partner who is living in or moving to a new country should get well-informed about all the laws of the land in which he or she will live.

- Although the partner who is from that country might be able to give some of that information, it is still wise to learn from other sources, such as from a library. Even the citizen might not always know the laws of his or her own land.

TO THINK AND TALK ABOUT (8)

Laws of the land

Exchange information about varying laws in your respective countries, and research corresponding laws about the following in the country where you live or expect to live:

• the right to work	• marriage rites, laws
• proof of identity	• divorce
• immigration, citizenship	• discipline of children
• right to vote	• freedom of religion
• visa and passport	• religious expression
• marriage registration	• religious conversion
• child discipline	• bribes or fraud
• financial care of parents	• dress, hair or make-up
• permission to purchase land	• care of elderly parents
• physical assault	• traffic and driving regulations
• sexual assault	• noise, curfews

Chapter 3   Merging the Materials

What parts of me/you will become parts of US?

When two artists work together, they will need to consult each other on which materials to use and then coordinate these materials somehow. The end-result will be a mixed media creation. Of the immense range of materials available to them, they each have their own preferences: One will prefer water color, the other oils; one will use brushes, the other a spatula; one will use paper or canvas, the other will use clay, and so on.

These artists bring not only different materials to the task. They each have their own particular styles, expertise, and their own unique interpretation or perspective of the world. It is important that they compare these materials, styles, and perspectives; collaborate with each other; and then decide how much of what materials they will use. This process involves ongoing re-negotiation which process, hopefully both will enjoy

Similarly, before two partners decide to create their life together, they must realize which parts of their own identity they are bringing into the relationship. Asking themselves *who am I?* and *what matters to me?* is just the beginning. Only then can they look at each other's cultural differences, take note, and compare. Only then can they decide which elements of their identity they will keep, lay aside, or merge.

As the two become closer to each other, their identity *as a couple* moves toward an identity of its own. The partner who is not aware of his or her own needs, likes, tastes, cultural interests, rules, gender role, beliefs and customs, or if he or she disregards or simply denies them totally for the sake of the other — that partner might wake up one day and say, "What have I done? I've given up the true *me!*"

This is what happened to a French female journalist who met an Asian Indian. They met in France, and then she joined him once he returned to India. She was fascinated by everything there, became a Hindu, dressed in saris, cooked Indian food, and learned to play the sitar. Ten years later, she realized that she wanted to find the "original me" again. It was as if her own culture suddenly reawakened. Not surprisingly, her partner felt as though he had lost the person he thought he had married.

On the following pages various aspects of culture are listed which most likely have influenced who you are today. Look at it from time to time. You might think of more than are on that list, and it might be that more insight and observations come to mind in the years to come.

The seesaw process of trying new things and wanting your own way is an inevitable part of the creative process. While gaining a great deal of new ideas, practices, tastes, and so forth from your partner, you might also experience a sense of loss as you give up or play down some of your own cultural beliefs, preferences, and practices. Perhaps some of your preferences simply don't fit in with those of your partner or with those of the culture in which you now live, and so you bravely lay yours aside — some permanently but some only temporarily.

TO THINK AND TALK ABOUT (9)

Cultural identity changes

Which aspects of my identity (for example, tastes, beliefs or practices) do I want my partner to adopt?
What parts of my partner's identity am I willing to accept or adopt?
What parts of my identity does my partner want me to give up or change?
What parts of my partner's identity do I want him/her to change?
What cultural parts of me do I revert to for comfort when I'm sad, angry, or frustrated?

Partners who are aware of their identity are more able to decide which aspects are important to them, and which are less so. They are then able to hold on to some of these aspects, even if the partner is quite different in these areas.

The first step, however, is to become more aware of the wide variety of aspects that form a person's identity. Many of these aspects are taken for granted until you notice that the partner's behavior and expectations are not the same as yours.

In the following pages some aspects of identity are listed:

- Ethnic and Family Roots — *my canvas or yours?*

- Basic needs — *an urge to be creative*

- Tastes and passions — *a variety of tools*

- Appropriate behaviors and traditions — *a variety of strokes*

- Values — *personal styles*

- World views — *two different palates*

- Religion — *two different colors*

- Other identity factors —

    o Education

    o Areas of significance

    o Political persuasions

    o Laws of the land

I   Ethnic and family roots: my canvas or yours?

Where do we each come from?

Who you are today is partially because you are a product of your family of origin: your parents, grandparents, great-grandparents, and the significant extended family members.

Ideally, you should be proud of your race and ethnicity. However, if you were born in a country where others have rejected you or hated you because of your race or ethnic background, you might have developed an inferiority complex or a defeatist attitude ("All my problems are because I'm _____"). You might think there is no hope for change, and you give up trying to improve your life, your relationships, or your surroundings. Or, by contrast, you might have developed a strong drive and effort to prove that you have intrinsic worth despite your background, and you are full of hope and ambition to change your life, your relationships, or your surroundings.

Yet a third response might be to look for a new society or land to identify with. This might include looking for a partner of another race or ethnic group, or a partner who lives in another country or comes from a totally different culture, but someone who totally accepts who you are — or at least tries to understand and accept who you are.

TO THINK AND TALK ABOUT (10)

My upbringing and family of origin

What am I proud of when I think of my ethnic origin?
What am I proud of when I think of my family heritage?
What circumstances or events shaped or influenced my grandparents and
my parents?
How did these circumstances or events affect them? How did these
circumstances affect me?
What were some of their basic values, beliefs and views that influenced me?
(Include moral laws, values, superstitions, mottos, world view, principles,
views about the opposite sex ...)
How did my parents discipline me and show me love?
How is my relationship with them now?
What place or role do I have among my siblings?
What am I most thankful for when I think of my upbringing?
What am I sad or angry about when I think of my family of origin?

2   Basic needs: an urge to be creative

What do we share in common?

"What drives me? What do I want in life? Why do I do what I do?" These
are questions everyone should ask at some point in their lives. The answers
partly lie in what many psychologists have coined "basic human needs." They
are as follows:

- security (physical survival, nourishment, shelter, safety)

- significance (feeling worthwhile, capable, having a role in society)

- love & belonging (family, friends, being loved by and loving others)

- freedom (independence, autonomy, privacy, your own "space")

- pleasure (fun, beauty, sensual pleasure, and enjoyment)

Everyone has these basic needs to some degree or another, but they raise
the following questions, "Are some of these needs more important than others
in my life at this time? If so, which ones?" and "How can I meet these needs?"

These questions are answered differently from person to person and from culture to culture.

When one partner views fun and pleasure as more important than food and shelter, and the other thinks the reverse, there is a conflict to resolve. When basking in the sun is pleasurable to one, but going to a concert is to the other, but both partners crave for togetherness, they could try to find a third activity that meets both their needs for pleasure and belonging. Or, if providing food for the family back home is as important to one partner as buying the ninth pair of jeans is to the other, a discussion ought to precede action.

These various priorities of needs might change at different times in a person's life, but they may also differ from culture to culture. In many Nigerian villages the need for love and belonging, as fulfilled in close family ties, takes on a higher importance than the need for individual freedom, privacy, or autonomy. In Germany's large cities it is usually the reverse. A wife from a Central American country expects her husband to go to a movie Friday night, while the husband from a North American country stays in the office late to compete with his co-workers for an increase in salary.

**In an intercultural partnership,
each partner has a different cultural perception
of which need is more important
and how each of these needs can be met.**

51

Many quarrels take place when either or both of the partners fail to understand or acknowledge the other's priority needs or the ways the other meets these needs. There are many variations on this theme! The need for freedom and independence for a family of five living in the Arctic might be fulfilled by an invisible barrier around one corner of an igloo; or for a single female student in Belgium, by a separate apartment three kilometers from the parents' house; or for a wealthy Italian, by a Ferrari. A woman might meet her need for significance as she cares and manages a household of four children, or directs a music school, or associates with someone who is very important. A man might meet this same need, for example, through his social status or his achievements in a sport event. Other men or women might find significance by providing for their families through a high-paying position in the company they work for; yet others see themselves equally as significant, no matter what they do or who they are.

TO THINK AND TALK ABOUT (11)

Basic needs

Rearrange the list of basic needs in the column below according to what you think is most important in your present circumstances.

- security (physical survival, nourishment, shelter, safety)

- significance (feeling worthwhile, having a role in society)

- love & belonging (loved by and loving family and friends)

- freedom (independence, autonomy, privacy)

- pleasure (fun, beauty, sensual pleasure, and enjoyment)

Which three needs are currently the most important to me?
How do we differ in the way we meet these needs?

---

3 Tastes and preferences: a variety of tools

How do we differ in what we like or dislike?

Each partner brings a different set of tools to the task of creating an art piece. Does that mean that neither can learn to appreciate or use those of the other? Of course not. Each partner learns to understand how the tastes and preferences of the other function, what good they can bring to the project, and how they can enrich the whole picture. In this process of interchange, each partner can also learn to use and enjoy the tools from the other, but only if they permit each other to do so! In an intercultural partnership, the possibilities of this interchange are endless.

Very often, sadly, partners allow their differences in tastes and preferences to become a reason for discouragement instead of a reason to celebrate. They "give up" on each other and work separately side-by-side, rather than integrate what they can each bring into the relationship. Instead of asking, "Why do I *not* like this?" they could ask, "How can I learn to like this? Or how can we use this to make our lives more interesting?"

Every culture has its own taste of what's fun, beautiful, and pleasurable, although there are some universal commonalities. Susan and Manuel are quite different from each other in interests and tastes. She loves to listen to a Bach concerto by blaring at 100 decibels in the living room every Sunday morning. He prefers to listen to jazz. How will they handle this? He could do his own thing, and she hers, which is easy with today's MP3 players and headphones. Or, she might coax him into staying in the living room with her and "learn to like her music," as she puts it. If he refuses, she is angry and disappointed. She doesn't give up, however, and the next time she tries to persuade him to listen with her, he gives in to her to keep the peace. She doesn't notice that he's bored, lonely, and isolated, and even worse, that he feels controlled by her.

There are other options: As long as the disinterested partner does not feel pushed into liking something or into joining the other in an activity, and as long as there is a mutual desire to be with each other, it might be very possible for the tastes of the one partner to "rub off on" or influence the other. Or perhaps, the partners could discover together a fusion that bridges both genres.

A student from Indian subcontinent was amused when she was in a middle class North American home as a guest. The home had five rooms, and in each room there was a television so that each person watched his or her own show. One watched a comedy, another a mystery, and still another, a sport event. She wondered when they did anything together. She learned that once a week, they rented a movie to watch together as a family taking turns in choosing a movie.

Food is another issue. Fortunately in many larger cities in the West, this is not a problem where fast food restaurants and ethnic grocery stores are in abundance. However, it can be a problem when the partner who cooks insists on his or her own cuisine and disregards the palate of the other.

> *After 10 years of curry smell in the house, I couldn't take it anymore. I sat down with my wife one day and told her. She cried. We made a deal: She cooks curry for three days and I eat out on those days. On three of the other days I cook European supper for both of us, but she eats lunch at her sister's house. And one day a week, I eat curried chicken with her! She's happy with that.*
>
> *– J. from Sweden*

It is impossible to force someone to enjoy something the same way you do. The more you try to persuade the other, the less likely he or she will learn to like it.

TO THINK AND TALK ABOUT (12)

Interests, tastes, hobbies, pastime

Name yours.

- sport — active, passive, what kind?
- music to listen to — active, passive, what kinds?
- dance — what kind?
- music performed — how, with whom, what kind?
- movies — what type?
- books — what type and how often?
- television programs — what type, when and how often or how long?
- visual beauty — what interior décor, architecture, flowers, colors?
- fashion — what clothes, hairstyles, colors?
- food — what kind? Cook yourself or eat out?

What about other interests, fascinations, tastes, passions?

What could we do together that we both enjoy?

What will you do with me that you don't enjoy?

What would I do with you that I don't enjoy?

What would or could I do alone? How would or does that affect our relationship?

---

4   Behaviors and customs: a variety of strokes

What do we do differently and how do we do them differently?

(a) Social rules and manners

As children we learned how to behave by mimicking the adults around us, and by rebuke and correction. Yet family rules and social expectations vary from culture to culture, especially how to relate to the opposite gender.

Friendliness (smiling and sparkling eyes) might be interpreted in one culture as an offer of friendship and in another as mere nervousness and shyness. In another, it could be seen as fake, and in yet another, as sexually willing. Quietness and a serious face could be interpreted as cold, distant, disinterested, or perhaps as proud; yet it could mean that the person is fearful, shy, or merely humble. A woman remaining seated after a meal to relax might be interpreted as laziness by some, or as an intrusion into male space by others. In some southern societies of the United States, a woman who does not constantly smile when talking to someone might be seen as hard, unfeminine, or even hostile.

TO THINK AND TALK ABOUT (13)

Social Rules and Manners

What was customary or allowed in your home or social group?
What do you find offensive in the culture of your partner?
How would you want your partner to behave when your family comes to visit?
How would my partner want me to behave when his/her family comes to visit?
How are the following different in my partner's culture?

- amount of physical distance between two colleagues standing and talking
- meeting strangers: how? when? where?
- greeting friends or relatives of the same sex; of the opposite sex: how?
- body posture in front of elders or superiors
- public displays of affection ("PDA") with your partner
- introducing friends to your partner and visa-versa
- friendliness: with whom and when?
- eye contact: who looks at whom and when?
- sitting or getting up or standing when?
- legs and feet position; hand gestures
- table manners: touching food when with which hand or utensils?
- spitting, belching, coughing, and sneezing in public
- gifts and gift giving, to whom, what, on which occasion?
- other taboos: (things not allowed to do in public)

A specific example of a difference in social rules concerns hospitality, which affects both hosts and guests. In Western cultures (especially in the larger cities), privacy of the immediate core family is valued highly; it is therefore usually not polite to visit someone unannounced or uninvited. Telephone calls and e-mails are enough of an intrusion in their busy lives! When an unexpected friend does appear at the door, the host might chat with that person standing at the door, and together they agree on an appointment for a longer visit another time. This is quite different in many other cultures where a surprise guest becomes a priority over every thing else and is treated royally, even with a hot meal.

TO THINK AND TALK ABOUT (14)

Hospitality

Exchange the customs you grew up with and compare with those that are acceptable in the country where you now live (or will live).

Hosting:
Whom do you like to host? When, how often and how long?
Do you invite people, or do you hope they come uninvited?
What do you serve and when?
After the guest says "No more, thank you," do you offer food and how often?
Do men and women sit and eat together when guests are present?
Where do the children eat when you have adult guests?
What do you expect your guests to bring when you invite them to a meal? If nothing, why?

Being a guest:
Can I come only when invited? Also without prior notice?
Should I come at the exact time the host said I should come?
Or am I expected later, and if so, how much later?
What do I bring to the host when invited? Should I ask?

Do I take off my shoes before entering the main part of the home?
Do I help myself to the food on the table or wait until it is offered?
How do I use a knife and fork in your country? Or do I at all?
Is burping forbidden, taboo, or encouraged?
What about slurping soup? Blowing my nose? Or …?
Must I say "no" when offered something, even if I really want it? How
many times should I refuse?
Am I allowed in the kitchen?
How do I show appreciation afterward?

(b) Rituals, traditions:

On a daily, weekly, and annual basis, each family has its own rituals and
patterns of living. Many conflicts could be avoided if partners can understand
and accept the importance of each other's certain family traditions and national
festivals. One partner might prefer to sleep in Sunday morning, while the other
attends an early morning mass, takes a jog, or goes for a swim. One wants to
watch a baseball game on television; the other prefers to take a walk. One might
like to surf in Hawaii during the holidays, while the other wants to go home to
Japan to see her family. All these things should be discussed well in advance to
avoid disappointments. Negotiation, re-negotiation, and compromises are always
in order!

National traditions, like Thanksgiving for Americans, or Anzac Day for New
Zealanders, as well as religious traditions, such as the Festival of Lights, Christmas,
or Eid, are not only different from one another, but they touch individuals at a
deeper level than personal or family rituals do. Often these collective traditions are
rooted in belief systems that participants are unaware of. In addition to following
some of these traditions, an intercultural couple can also think and talk about
creating their own traditions, or incorporate some traditions of both partners.

TO THINK AND TALK ABOUT (15)

Rituals and holiday traditions

Compare some traditions or rituals that each of you wishes to incorporate into
this relationship, and state specifically how you like to observe them.

- holiday celebrations (which ones? what do you want to continue to
  observe even if you live in another country?)

- morning, noon, and evening rituals

- days off from work or weekends

- birthdays, anniversaries (how celebrated? what do you expect from your partner?)

- birth rites, coming-of-age rites, death of a loved one

- vacations or longer work holidays (how spent? where and with whom?)

- fasting, certain food restrictions during special times

- sleeping, resting (when, how long?)

- other rituals or traditions

Then ask yourself and each other:

- How can we compromise on who does what, when, and how often?

- Which activities do we do alone and which together?

---

5   Values and worldview: The *why* question

Why do we do things differently?

Each of us as individuals has a personality that is unique. Researchers are still debating as to how much of our personality is shaped by our genes, but they agree that at least a part of who we are is influenced by the total sum of our experiences.

One of the ways we all learn from our environment is through what we hear: the spoken word. Another way we learn is through what we see and observe, such as by interacting with our family and with the community in which we grow up. By what we hear and see, we absorb the corresponding worldview, values, practices, and beliefs, which then influence who we become as adults.

The sum total of these learned experiences varies from group to group, clan to clan, and family to family. For instance, a person might view the questions of another as far too direct and expects the other to observe first before asking. Another might make long to-do lists of day-to-day demands yet never call his close relatives to see how they are. Some might ask, "How do you feel today?" as a form of greeting; they don't expect the responding person to bare open his or her soul or to share the deep things of the heart. Merely a quick, "Fine, thank you," would do as an answer, regardless of how the responder really feels. Anything more honest than that might actually be inappropriate.

These various approaches to communication affect not only a marriage partnership, but also how hospitals are run, how government offices conduct themselves, how children are taught in school, and more. As a general rule, people are unaware of why they do things the way they do them, or why they relate to others a certain way. When they come into conflict with another person, they have no idea as to why. They don't know that their behaviors and words are influenced by a unique set of values, and that those values are influenced by a unique set of beliefs. When the values and beliefs differ from those of another person, the resulting behaviors are different.

**The less aware we are of each other's
different values and worldviews,
the more we become prime targets for misunderstandings.**

**The more aware we are of each other's
different values and worldviews,
the less there will be misunderstandings.**

(a) Values

Our values are the basis for why certain behaviors are important to us. In each culture these values are woven together in a unique way. To find out the underlying values that dictate your own behavior, or why this behavior is important to you, you need to ask yourself a sequence of at least three questions:

- Why do I do a certain thing in a particular way?

- Why did I give that answer?

- And why did I give that reason for that answer?

Here is an example of this thought process. The wife thinks: "I love it when my husband thanks me for making him dinner." *Why?* "Because I want to be appreciated for all the hard work I have done." *Why?* "Because I don't like doing hard work, but I try hard to please him anyway." *Why?* "Because if I have to do the hard things, I need someone to thank me for it." *And why is that important to me?* "I need someone to make me feel worthwhile. And I only feel worthwhile when I am appreciated by somebody else."

The husband thinks: "I do not thank her for making me a meal because I do not think that thanking her is necessary." *Why?* "Because as my wife she has the duty to do for me what I require of a wife." *Why?* "Because a good wife is an honor to her husband, not only in the home, but also in society. She frees me to live well in the community." *Why?* "Because I value being honored by other men when they hear I have a good wife."

Many books have been written on this subject for business people whose goal is to make lots of money in different cultures. (See Further Reading in Appendix III). The same principles used in that context can be applied to all intercultural relationships.

TO THINK AND TALK ABOUT (16)

Underlying values

For each of the following pairs, identify which part is more important to you in what situations, and then compare with your partner.

- the wishes and needs of a group, or those of an individual
- spiritual well-being or material wealth
- relationships or the production/acquisition of things or money
- the process or the end product
- locks and boundaries, or open doors
- beauty or practicality
- quantity or quality
- relationships, or cleanliness and order
- saving face or honest criticism
- handling one thing at a time or many things at once

When do you or don't you fight for what is right?
When and by whom is aggressive, loud interaction acceptable?
How is power shared or measured? By age, wealth, position, or — ?
When does admitting to failure appear weak? When is it strong?
Which of the following do you think you have to be to survive

- courageous, self-confident, or passive, and carefree
- cautious, suspicious, or trusting and determined
- aggressive, selfish, forward, or non-assertive, giving and selfless?
- always friendly or serious?

Before exchanging answers with your partner, ask yourself the following:
What differences in values have I noticed already?
Can I accept the different values of my partner?
Can we live harmoniously and in peace despite these differences?
Which of my values am I willing to change to please my partner?

(b) Worldview

A worldview *is* the sum-total of deep convictions which influence how we think and how we prioritize our lives. If someone else challenges any of these convictions, a deep emotional reaction occurs even though we might not even know why. The four key areas of our broad view of the world include our view of man, our view of nature, our view of the supernatural, and our view of time, plus the interactions of these. These views are founded and supported and passed on to us through folktales and myths, through religion, through the authoritative teaching of those we love and respect, through family, or through drama and rituals.

"It is exactly one hour before the concert begins. That means we have 10 minutes to get dressed, 3 minutes to put on your shoes and coat, 4 minutes to get into the car, 10 minutes to drive there, 10 minutes to find a parking space, another 5 to park the car, 8 minutes to walk to the concert hall, 5 minutes to check in our coats, and 5 more minutes to find our seats before the concert starts at promptly 8:00 PM."

- Our view of man: Is man essentially good, evil, neutral, or suspect? Does he exist just to be or is he on earth to be active, to control the world, or to develop his inner person? Are his relationships with other people primarily based on leading or being led, on controlling others or being controlled by others, or on the need of others or an obligation to be there for others? Is competition more important than cooperation? Are the chief goals in life desires for profits or for wisdom? Are all people created equal, or are certain races, people groups, women, or outsiders less equal than others?

- Our view of nature: Is nature to be wondered at and respected, or feared? Is it possible to control our natural environment to our advantage, and if so, to what extent? Is it our role to submit to its forces and strengths? Are natural disasters inevitable or can mankind and/or a supernatural being influence them? Do scientific developments shape our morals?

- Our view of the supernatural: What part does the supernatural play in our view of reality? Is the whole world divided and ranked into two tiers that include gods and the physical world — persons, animals and nature — or is there a third tier in between in which the spirit world might interfere? If so, are the spirits powerful sources of evil and good, and must they be appeased? Are we humans supposed to appease the needs and wishes of a higher being? Is there a God who cares enough to die for those he loves? What are the sources of our morality and our responsibility for life?

- View of time: All mankind lives with the past, a present and a future, but which is most important and when? Do you forget the past, strive for reconciliation, or perpetuate the past? Does time keep you or do you keep time? To some, there is no need to think much about how things were done in the past, because what we do now affects the future, and the future is in fact more important than the present. Others are not at all concerned about the future, because who knows what will happen next? No use planning ahead! Still others value the past, especially the experiences of past generations; they say, "If it works, don't change it."

- View of knowledge: Our thoughts and ideas about what is affect what we do. But how do we know what is? Does some or all knowledge come to us directly from the supernatural, from the womb, or from God? Was the knowledge always there and we simply "remembered" it? Or is knowledge always attained through observation and scientific proof? What counts more — the instinctive wisdom of mothers, or today's books on childrearing?

There are other aspects of worldview, such as how we view history and the future of mankind and the earth. Discussions surrounding them can be endless, but most importantly, the way we answer them eventually directs our behavior and goals.

For an intercultural marriage to work,
each partner must to some degree
learn to understand, acknowledge, and respect
the views of the other partner,
even if they cannot come to some agreement.

TO THINK AND TALK ABOUT (17)

Worldview

Is man essentially good, evil, neutral or suspicious?
Does the spirit world control my life lives?
How do I view nature: to be respected, used or protected?
Which is more important and when: past, present or future?
How does my view of time influence the way I live?
What purpose does suffering have?
What is real? Can I know what is real if cannot see or touch it?
Am I more, less, or equally important than my fellow human beings?
Are love, sacrifice, happiness, and sorrow real or imagined?
Is this life I now have the only one I'll have, or is there more?

---

6   Religion - the spiritual dimension in practice

What higher authority rules and guides me?

Views concerning religion and different religious beliefs are an important aspect of worldview. They affect whether people follow certain rituals, to what extent, how often, where, and when. They also provide a framework for what people consider as right or wrong.

Not only do religious views themselves vary, but also the extent of agreement with and commitment to them. Level of commitment could vary from "it matters a lot to me" to "it is really of no interest." Some are committed to a *personal* faith; others delight in the drama and ritual; and still others are zealously involved in its *political* affiliation. Some only consider themselves *nominal* adherents; that is, they identify with a certain religion by name only, but not in faith or practice.

Whether they realize it or not, many people are still influenced by their religious upbringing, by the ethics, principles, and rules that their families in past generations followed, and by the moral and ethical rules that are by-products of the dominant religion(s) in their country.

"His parents were very nice to me until he asked me to marry him."

When partners of two different cultures share the same religious faith and practice, and if they are equally committed to that faith, their other cultural issues might be easier to handle. Perhaps their united faith offers a spiritual strength and practical help which can help them overcome any trials they might have. If this faith is the *only* aspect the couple has in common, the cultural differences that remain could make life so miserable that their anger and frustration could lead to a weakening of that faith.

> *When he was praying about whether or not we should get engaged, a melody went through my boyfriend's head with the words, "No turning back, no turning back." We took this to be divine guidance and married. Afterward we realized how different we were in every aspect except our faith, and I began to doubt that it was God who spoke to us through that song. But then I thought, if it wasn't God, then there would be no point to our marriage. And if it really was God, there must be a reason. We're still waiting to find out what that is.*
>
> *– G. from Singapore*

Marrying someone from a different faith would be unthinkable to many who regard their faith as a top priority in their identity and in their society. In some cases, interfaith marriages go against their religious principles or rules; in other cases they invite rejection by one or both families.

Religious differences between partners might also pose the following problems:

- When important rituals cannot be shared: For both religious and secular people, beliefs offer explanations for suffering and evil, the reason for existence, or the purpose of life, and they offer guidelines for relating to the natural and the supernatural world. These beliefs influence rituals surrounding birth, weddings, and death — three key religious occasions in which families get together. If one of the partners cannot or will not share in these beliefs and rituals, the other experiences a marked feeling of something missing in the relationship.

- When stress causes a partner to go extreme: Whether tensions come from inside or outside the relationship, one of the partners might revert more and more to his or her original cultural values, world views, customs, tastes, and behavior, and sometimes to an even more rigid form of his or her religion than before the relationship began. In fact, this partner might become more of the person he or she was originally before the relationship began. For example, a not very devout Muslim, who, prior to marrying, did not observe Ramadan before the wedding suddenly decides it is important to do so. Another example might be a secular humanist who suddenly doesn't want any religious influence in the house. This new fervor might cause the other partner to feel left out, pressured, or abandoned. The result? More tension between the partners, and finally, if unresolved, the possibility of drifting apart.

- When the spouse or partner tries to persuade the other to convert: It is normal for people who are enthusiastic about what they believe to share their personal persuasion with others, especially with a partner they want to be intimate with. The partner might be either willing to listen, or he might not at all be interested. A perfectly normal but lively interchange can follow in which one partner defends her view, or even argues or protests against the views of the other. A decision to convert from one religion to another is, at least in many countries, permissible.

Keep the following in mind:

When the partner says he feels harassed or pushed, or when he becomes irrationally defensive, it is time to stop sharing one's faith and bringing up the topic. On the other hand, it is perfectly legal, ethical, and healthy to exchange views on matters such as religion, or to ask each other honest questions, as long as both partners are willing to do so.

When one partner makes a quick decision to convert just to please or win the other partner, that so-called conversion might not last. Unless that person has first examined his or her own religious upbringing as well as that of the partner, and unless he or she understands both religions well, he or she cannot really make an honest decision.

If religious laws require that the husband maintain custody of the children after divorce, his foreign wife might convert in order to maintain access to the children and some inheritance.

- When a parent of either spouse expects the other to convert: It is worthwhile to look not only at your partner's religious formation but also at the faith of his or her parents. Parents can be dominant and powerful, especially if they are wealthy and offer an inheritance, or if they are deeply committed to their beliefs. In Shintoism and Catholicism, the parents' welfare in life after death might depend on certain rites their offspring do on their behalf. Their wish to see those carried out is understandable and might place a lot of pressure on their children.

- When there are children: Some partners who have different religious affiliations yet live harmoniously together allow their children to decide for themselves which religion they should follow. If parents choose to provide religious teaching, how they do so depends on their view of upbringing. Is it one of self-discovery, allowing the child to explore and learn on their own? Or, is it one of guidance with the admonition, "Let me show you so you won't make a mistake?" Or is it a little of both? In some cases one parent will insist the children be given full teaching in his faith. Sometimes it is the caretaking grandparents who decide the matter.

If the children feel pulled apart by parents and grandparents on this issue, they might end up disinterested in religion altogether. Alternatively they might choose the faith of one parent or the other for whatever reason. This could cause much family confusion, arguments, and ridicule, unless the parents model an attitude of tolerance. Some couples, however, expose their children to no religious faith at all.

- When grown children marry someone from another religion: Parents of adult children who have fallen in love with someone from another religion often realize that despite their wishes and warnings, they cannot ultimately control their grown children. When Singh from northern India fell in love with Anna from Karalla, India, his parents asked Anna to consider converting to his family's faith. Her reply was that she would like to take ten years to study both of their religious texts, and then she would give her answer. In the meantime she would let the children be trained in the Sikh religion but she would also have the freedom to live out her faith in front of them. The parents respected this promise and approved of the marriage. When, ten years later, Anna decided to remain in her own faith, her husband's family honored her decision.

In summary, interfaith relationships can only work well under the following conditions:

- if the respective religion of the partners is not as important to them as other unifying factors;

- if the guilt-shame factor for going against the wishes or rules of their religious authority does not pose a problem;

- if the extended family of the one partner does not interfere in any way or openly rejects the other partner;

- if the extended family of the one parent doesn't make fun of, complain to, put pressure on, or ridicule the other parent in front of them;

- if the laws of the country do not favor one faith over the other; and

- if the extended family doesn't try to influence one or more of the children against the expressed permission of the parents.

TO THINK AND TALK ABOUT (18)

Religious beliefs and morals

Compare your views with those of your partner and note where you agree.

If the spirit world or a higher being controls our lives, what is my role or duty in the partnership?

What do I believe about an after-life?

What are my beliefs about birth? Death? Suffering?

What do I believe about the role of good and evil in the world?

What is my religion's attitude towards women?

What is my religion's attitude towards the elderly? Towards family?

Who are my current religious leaders or source of authority? Do I follow them? To what extent?

How do I rid myself of shame and guilt?

What is my responsibility towards others?

What rituals do I do when, how often, where?

How do my religious beliefs differ from my partner? from his/her family?

Am I open to changing my current convictions about religion, or do I currently believe that I would never change them?

Then ask:

Which of the above beliefs influence your behavior today?

How would our differences in these views impact our life together?

---

7   Other identity factors

What from my background affects how I live?

(a) Education

Education is not just a matter of degrees and titles but also of attitude and mind. Many people are self-educated and can carry on a more intelligent conversation about many different topics than those who have a specialized degree in one field. Others might not have an academic degree, but they have skills and knowledge that enable them to produce many practical things with their hands or to succeed in business or in the world of arts and crafts.

In some environments, particularly in cities, it is perfectly normal for the woman to have a higher degree of education than her husband. In other cultures, this would be unthinkable.

High and dry but rooted

What a very strange picture of a tree. A few years ago it would not have been like this: the pond beside which it was growing had since drained away, and it was left high and dry!

It looks funny to us, but the tree coped. Its roots followed the water level, down, down, down… and so it has continued to live and flourish.

Living in new and unfamiliar circumstances just might feel as *if the water is draining away.*

**In time, as your roots will go deeper,
you will find a new and local source of strength.**

Perhaps, even years after the marriage, such as when the children are grown up or when finances allow, one of the partners, perhaps the wife, might wish to further her education. If such an opportunity is possible in the country where the family lives, this choice could change the balance in the relationship. It could also affect either the home-bound status of the wife and her contribution to family life. It could also affect the attitude of her partner. If he focuses on her wishes and goals rather than his own felt needs and expectations, and if he shares in her joy and excitement, *her* adventure can also become *their* adventure. It would mean adjustments, sacrifices, and many changes on both sides. The end result could be a brand new appreciation of each other.

TO THINK AND TALK ABOUT (19)

Education background and goals

Does my partner accept the educational level I have achieved?
If not, what does he or she expect me to achieve?
Do I accept the educational level my partner has achieved?
Is my partner open to seeking more education later on?
Would I encourage or support his or her educational goals for the future?
What would be my reaction if he or she failed or gave up?

(b) Pride versus humility

To feel significant on this planet earth is not the same as being prideful or conceited, or as viewing oneself as better than or more important than others. Some individuals see themselves as created and even designed by God for his enjoyment, and that alone makes them feel significant, even if others in life demean or humiliate them. They don't see themselves as *more* valuable than others, but treat others with *equal* respect, helping others feel as valuable as they themselves do.

How persons express their own value in relation to others differs from culture to culture, and can often be misinterpreted. For example, a North America compliments his partner from the Ukraine for her beauty. When she answers, "Oh, no, I'm not beautiful at all," the North American might think with disdain, "Oh! She has a very low opinion of herself." But according to her cultural protocol, she wants to show that she is humble and not overly prideful or conceited. If this were in reverse, that is, if the

Ukrainian complimented the American, who, in turn, responded with a confident "Thank you!" — the Ukrainian might think of the American as being arrogant.

TO THINK AND TALK ABOUT (20)

What makes me valuable in my world?

Ask yourself and each other, which of the following make you feel important:

- present or desired career
- social status or role
- talents, abilities, recognition, and awards
- being a member of my family
- role or status in my family
- role in a club, church, or in the community
- being a citizen of a particular country

List some other sources of what would make you feel important in the future

- future hopes, dreams, goals for me? (career, property, status, etc.)
- future hopes, dreams, goals for my partner?
- future hopes, dreams, goals for my children?
- alternative plans in case these dreams are not fulfilled?
- if these goals are not fulfilled, what else could make me feel valuable?

(c) Political viewpoints and involvement

It is natural for people to be interested in the politics or certain policies of their own country. However, in an intercultural relationship, it is good to be aware of the political climate and policy changes in the partner's country as well. If the partner's country of origin is at peace after a period of war, it might mean that he or she wants to return there at least for a visit. If the partner's country is under threat of war or at war, there is the constant worry about relatives and friends who are experiencing difficult times. A visit to that country might not be advisable or safe. The degree of commitment to a partner's country of origin and his or her involvement in political affairs might eventually affect the safety of both partners and the lives of the children.

One question which would be fair to exchange and answer honestly is, "What is more important to me: My family's safety or the defense of my political beliefs?"

TO THINK AND TALK ABOUT (21)

Governments and politics

Name or list some political issues in your current country you both agree on, such as:

- types of government and political systems
- political party of preference
- the problem of poverty and the homeless
- your country's attitude toward certain other countries and vice versa
- wars past and current, military service, nationalism, willingness to fight or die for one's country or political cause.

Can you and your partner honestly exchange opinions without fear of being rejected or laughed at, or without being punished or put in danger?

Chapter 4   Devising the Design

Do our goals match?

If you and your partner have decided to partner together and perhaps even to produce a family together, you are about to begin to work on what will be like a huge, never-finished "art project" that requires much detailed planning. Imagine if one partner wanted to create a large abstract painting, and the other a detailed miniature! Or if the two artists never talked about their goals, yet proceeded to work on the same canvas! Two artists working on one piece of art must decide together the size of canvas they will use, the tools and palette they will bring, the climate they want to work in, and the colors they will use.

The same is true in real-life partnership: What if one partner views the relationship as a life commitment, but the other does not? Or what if one partner wants a platonic, open relationship, and the other wants an exclusive marriage? To avoid disappointment and even greater conflicts ahead, it would be wise to discuss the long-term goals of the relationship early on. But the discussion should not end there. Once the basic goals are agreed upon, the partners should engage in an ongoing, never-ending process of making, matching, mending, and meeting new goals.

Never assume anything.
Don't take for granted that your partner knows
what you want or expect.
Don't wait until fate decides your life.
Avoid the shock of
having your dreams different from what you expected.

I Initial formalities

How will we symbolize our commitment?

Many relationship therapists and psychologists believe that true intimacy in a relationship can take place only if there is a life commitment to that relationship. As long as one partner is not sure what the other intends for the relationship, the ensuing uncertainty might lead to mistrust, which in turn might lead to quarrels, heightened tension, lessened sexual satisfaction, and ultimately, early separation.

The questions below are therefore important to ask:

- What do you wish that your partner would do or say to show that he or she is committed exclusively to you for life?

- What will you do or say that your partner can be sure that you are committed to him or her for life?

The way you answer the above questions might be very different from the way someone from another culture answers them.

In the Western world, an increasing number of couples choose not to marry with ceremony or with legal recognition, and choose to simply live together. Some couples do this to save on the costs of a wedding and possible divorce. However, surveys have shown that for many such couples, the individual partners feel less secure in the relationship, less committed to each other, and less determined to make it last.

In many non-Western countries, such live-in relationships are disdained. Even in those countries where cohabiting couples are accepted by society, these couples might not enjoy the same rights as the ones accorded to married couples. In many places their offspring might suffer ridicule or rejection. If there is a frequent change of partners, children will feel less secure and will have a more complicated self-identity.

Poverty, civil unrest, or other extreme circumstances might prevent the couple from having a public, civil, or religious ceremony. Therefore, in some countries, states, or provinces, partners who have lived together for a long period of time and who publicly declare that they are married are then considered legally married. The required time of cohabitation varies from place to place.

However, in most cultures there is some sort of public ceremony along with a private pledge that expresses the commitment. Here are some examples.

(a) Engagement

The *engagement* (or sometimes called *betrothal*) is a formal declaration that a certain man and a certain woman are to be married. In some cultures it is merely a preparation and planning time for an upcoming or later wedding ceremony, and can be broken without shame. In other cultures, it is a formal celebration which is considered a firm contract of purchase and/or provision, a sacred vow not to be broken, and/or a license to have sexual consummation. To break this contract is shameful, especially for the woman, for it might affect her future prospects.

In some cultures the man must ask the father of his girlfriend for permission to marry her, after which there is an engagement party. As a symbol of their commitment, the man then gives the woman a piece of expensive jewelry (such as a gold band or ring). In many other cultures, both exchange such a gift.

(b) Marriage

The engagement period usually leads up to another formal, public commitment ceremony or celebration called a wedding. This event needs to be managed carefully if both families are involved. Whether public or private, a marriage ceremony formalizes or legalizes the beginning of a new social unit, with the man and wife committed to each other for life. A public ceremony and celebration give the family, friends, and in some cases, the whole community an opportunity to share in the festivities, to provide the couple with emotional and moral support, and to give them a head-start on some material goods.

There are many variations from country to country, and state to state, as to how a marriage is legalized. In some places, the civil legalization is automatic after a religious celebration; in others, an extra civil ceremony is required; and in still other places, a form is signed in the presence of witnesses. In the case of an intercultural marriage, it is wise to check whether such a legalized marriage is compatible with the laws of both passport countries, especially if the one wants to visit in the other's country of origin.

In many parts of the world, a religious ceremony gives a couple the feeling that the vow they make to each other is witnessed by a supernatural being or beings. In the monotheistic faiths, this would be God. Such a couple feels not only more blessed or empowered but also more obligated to stay true to those vows. Or the ceremony simply follows a tradition expected by the parents and community, either out of honest respect, or with the hidden hope to inherit the family's wealth.

In many countries, a *civil ceremony* (with a notary public official or lawyer who "officiates" the wedding and signs a marriage certificate) offers legal benefits and protection to each partner in case the other partner divorces, dies, or is unfaithful or negligent. In certain other countries, marriage reduces costs such as health insurance and taxes. It also provides some safety and security for some who become financially dependant on their partner at some point in the future.

A challenge in preparing a wedding ceremony of their own would be to balance both sets of religious beliefs and traditions. In some cases two ceremonies are held. In any case it would be honorable to reflect both traditions and include both languages for the sake of family and guests.

Marriage in some cultures is not complete until the woman is pregnant or bears a child; in others it is formalized by a dowry (a monetary payment from one family to another). An expensive piece of jewelry (such as a gold band or ring) is sometimes given or exchanged to symbolize the value of the relationship and their pledge to remain true to each other.

TO THINK AND TALK ABOUT (22)

Engagement and wedding protocol

In your family, how is an engagement properly celebrated?
Will there be a legal marriage-contract regarding finances?
When is sex permissible or expected? Before or after the engagement, before or after the civil or church wedding ceremony, or — ?
What are some of the pre-wedding rituals in your culture?

If you were to marry publicly, where would it be?

Who and how many will you invite? Will there be a special reception for all who attend, and/or another for relatives and special friends?

Who will pay for the wedding costs? How much is the budget?

What wedding presents are expected and when?

Which cultural tradition will dominate or how will both be expressed?

Which language(s) will be used in the ceremony? What music will be played?

Who dances with whom?

What physical contact may take place?

Will alcoholic drinks be allowed at the wedding reception/party?

How long will the bride and groom have to stay with the relatives and friends?

Are there any other customs or rituals expected?

---

2   The importance of commitment

Staying on task

Do wedding ceremonies — whether religious, social, or civil — guarantee a permanent relationship? Of course not. Yet similar to an employment contract, such ceremonies normally provide a solid foundation, order, structure, and discipline that many humans need in order to behave more responsibly, especially when the feelings of love fluctuate or diminish. In the West, many young adults are afraid of marrying because their parents were divorced, and they are afraid of the same mistake. Yet even if a couple never marries, a separation could cause just as much pain to their children as a divorce would.

Security of attachment is a vital element of intimacy, say many psychologists. But how can a woman feel secure when she is not sure whether the man has decided to be with her for the rest of his life? How can two pieces of wood stay together without nails, glue, or wire? The answer to both questions: They cannot.

**Commitment is more than the passive state
of two pieces of wood bound together with strong glue;
it is a willful decision that leads a couple
to feel more secure with each other.**

(a) What commitment *is*

Commitment makes people *feel* secure because they *know* they are secure. This knowledge and resulting feeling make it easier for partners to become intimate emotionally as well as sexually, and therefore to enjoy the relationship more. *Commitment* is defined[3] as *the state of being bound emotionally or intellectually to a course of action or to another person or persons.* Commitment involves accepting the reality of the sum total of what makes up each partner: his or her childhood, family of origin, weaknesses and strengths, failures and successes.

A relationship that will positively influence future generations needs to be based on more than just a feeling of love and warmth. This feeling might come and go, even in successful relationships. Studies show that while the "in love" feelings contribute much to the early adjustment phase and child production, it is the commitment to each other that ultimately leads to growing intimacy and well-adjusted offspring.

A commitment is often expressed in a vow during some marriage ceremonies. A vow is much stronger than a mere promise or resolution, which can easily be broken or unfulfilled. Vows have two aspects: an acknowledgement that both partners are human and might therefore fail, and a pledge that they draw strength from the mercy and grace of God. Such a vow is the one certainty that they do have, and it encourages them to make amends. A vow retains its power and validity, irrespective of conduct.

(b) What commitment *is not*

Commitment is not the same as passive resignation. It never gives the partner the license or right to abuse, misuse, or harm the partner — physically, sexually, verbally, or emotionally. Let's say a wife lives with a husband who constantly subjects her to resentful, snide, and demeaning remarks. Yet she passively endures out of fear or out of blind obedience, responses which might invite even more abuse from the husband. Instead, commitment calls for action when there is injustice, such as finding a safe place for shelter and insisting that the partner gets professional counseling.

(c) A word about divorce and other options

Unless the personal security and health of one partner or the children are at risk, separation, divorce, or looking for another partner does not necessarily solve the problem of a couple's unhappiness. Parents can hurt their children just as much, if not more, by divorcing than by exposing them to ongoing strife in the

[3] American Heritage® Dictionary of the English Language, Fourth Edition, 2000 by Houghton Mifflin Co.

home. Divorced partners who have children must face a continuing relationship between them as parents. Children will suffer less when the separated or divorced parents agree to disagree in a friendly, civil manner, and to co-operate with each other in the care of their children.

A word of advice before you divorce: Research the laws regarding access to your children, such as visitation rights, if they are taken away from you. Some countries have strict rules relating to foreign partners. Never sign divorce papers unless you have first consulted with a legal advisor or lawyer familiar with international law.

> *My girls were 5 and 7 when my husband decided to divorce me and send me home with the girls. I was so depressed at the time that I didn't know how to defend myself. A friend of mine brought me to a legal advisor who saw to it that my husband had to pay for the support of the children even after I left the country to go home to mine.*
>
> *-T. from Kenya*

(d) Afraid of commitment?

If adults today find themselves afraid of commitment or marriage, they should ask each other: "What are you afraid of exactly?" Usually such fears come as a result of past relationships that have gone sour. They just don't want to be hurt again. Or they remember the pain when their parents separated or divorced, and they vowed never to bring such pain to their children. Or they are afraid of getting close to someone but without understanding why.

Life is full of risks. From the moment you step out of bed, have something to eat, breathe the air, eat breakfast, drive to work, all is a risk — even when you go to sleep in your bed at night. It is said, the only thing certain in life is uncertainty.

Yes, commitment is a risk. So what? Why allow your fears to rob you of the joy you could have with each other?

Commitment is a lifelong project.
Creating a future together,
producing a family together,
and building a life together
will influence generations to come.

We live in a country where we have the freedom to divorce. That means we are not each other's prisoner or slave. My wife is legally and physically free to leave me. That's why I am less tempted to take advantage of her or to disrespect her. And I value her a lot for choosing to stay with me!

– R. from the Netherlands

Sometimes I feel that I can manage without my wife, and she without me. Then I remember the vow we made to each other before God on our wedding day. I remember her positive qualities and write her a thank you poem. She doesn't always respond right away, but when she does, it is worth the trouble!

– B. from England

3   Intimate minds and hearts

What dimensions do we plan to use?

What does being intimate really mean? Is it only a sexual union? Or is it a sexual union plus a business arrangement where each person has a practical role to fulfill?

By the word *intimate*, the authors mean much more than that.

The words *intimate* or *intimacy* can also refer to an emotional and mental closeness, as in "soul mates," for example. In some traditions such as in India, the Arab world, and Japan, the satisfaction of the emotional aspect of intimacy is not usually found in marriage but rather with members of one's own gender. For many in the Christian and Jewish traditions, however, the mind and the emotions are sought-after elements of desired intimacy (as in *Song of Solomon*, the Bible). Both Western and Eastern legends, stories, poetry, and dramas have expressed a longing for such intimacy for centuries, and attempts at finding it are made every day.

What does partnership look like when a man and a woman share their life, minds, emotions, and bodies together?

- It is a growing bond, an openness, acceptance and trust between two souls (heart or emotions, mind, and spirit) that want to get to know and value each other more and more.

- It is exclusive. It is possible to have many good and close friends, but being loved by someone and loving someone who is "all and only mine" is a very special relationship.

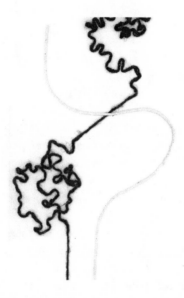

The challenge of change is not the same for both

Wool and string are really quite similar aren't they? They both come in lengths and are thin and round. It is possible to knit with both but can you imagine using wool to send a parcel through the post?

This wool had been part of a boy's sweater and the string had been used in the garden. So in their own ways they had been very useful and started to be molded quite differently. Even so, the wool can be straightened and it is still soft and flexible but it will never be strong. The string is still strong and tough: but it will always be too coarse for a baby's cardigan.

**Expect of yourself and your partner
what is reasonably possible.**

- It is a bond between two bodies, a gift of the body of one to the body of another, and this gift is pleasurable to both.

- Intimacy is sometimes a scary adventure. It is not always peaceful, but its end goal is to know and accept each other for who each one is.

When partners share with each other their honest thoughts, feelings, hopes, and dreams without fear of rejection, and when they can do so without the listener reacting in mockery, ugly retorts, a moralistic rebuke, or physical abuse, it could be said that they are intimate, or at least, growing in intimacy.

However, when one partner makes a hurtful remark toward the other, or laughs at him or her, the other partner naturally withdraws out of fear of being hurt again. The first then interprets this withdrawal as indifference and stops sharing intimate thoughts or feelings altogether. Eventually, both partners end up withdrawing from each other more and more. Their intimacy is diseased!

However, when intimacy between two partners *seems* to be lost, the opposite might actually be true. When a conflict erupts or when anger is used to release tensions, some partners panic. "Oh no! It's all over between us," they whine. True, their relationship is not as they had imagined it to be, but it is far from over. It would only be *really* finished if both gave up sharing their true feelings and thoughts from then on.

Conflicts might highlight the differences in a couple, but they only *seem* to prevent the couple from becoming more intimate. In fact, conflicts, including the expression of anger — though sometimes painful — can serve to *strengthen* the intimacy and oneness that a couple longs for. The following steps show how emotional and mental intimacy can grow despite and through conflicts:

- When you disagree with something the partner has said or done, find a quiet, non-rushed, peaceful moment soon afterward and begin by saying, "I think what you said or did was not right. I felt badly (or a more specific emotion) because ..." or, "Do you want to hear what I think about that?"

- Don't attack the person. Don't use the words, "You are ..." or "You always ..."

- Keep your voice calm and collected. An angry voice either ignites anger or causes your partner to withdraw or become defensive.

- In response to an honest but fair confrontation, say (and mean it!), "I hear what you are saying. I am sorry you feel this way. I was wrong when I ..... Please forgive me. What would you like me to do or say to make it right?"

- Even if your partner finds it hard to forgive you, make an honest attempt to change anyway.

Ask yourselves: What kind of partnership are you looking for? Do you want to get to know each other better, body, soul, and heart? Do you want to offer each other space and the place to do this?

**Each day for the rest of our lives
intimacy of mind, soul and spirit is an adventure.
It is always in danger!**

4 Power plays and negotiation skills

Whose colors will dominate and when?

When picturing man and woman, husband and wife, father and mother, parents and children — we usually imagine each combination as a pair of opposites in balance. Then when we add to this so-called balance different varieties of role expectations and culture-specific as well as gender-specific values, this image becomes more complex. Why? Because interactions within these relationships *are* extremely complicated!

To the questions of who leads and makes decisions in which areas, and which role each partner assumes, there is no one answer in all cultures. In some cultures and families, the man determines how the family income is spent; in others, the woman holds the family purse (See section 6, below). In some cultures the woman has total control over the discipline and education of the children; in others, the father does. In some, the husband would expect the wife to abandon her country, political persuasions, food preferences, religion, and customs, and to completely adopt his, regardless of where they live. In others, the family elder on the man's side of the family has a final say in all matters.

Still, in other cultures there is constant collaboration; that is, the partners discuss and decide who is in charge of what. They decide on these role definitions together, and they base this decision on who is best able and available to do what. Working out these roles between them requires a lot of patience and communication.

Sometimes power roles might change during the time between the start of the relationship and the marriage. It might change again, however, if and when the couple moves from one country to another. The partner in whose country the couple resides might take on a leadership role and appear controlling or "lording it over" the partner who is new to that culture. This behavior can be frightening to someone who accustomed to equality and independence.

> *When we were first married and were living in the United Kingdom, my wife taught me how to shop and cook the English way, and she took care of most of the banking and money management. She also decorated and furnished the house the way she saw fit, and she disciplined and taught the children. She was definitely the boss in matters of daily life, while I remained the initiator and she the faithful compliant in our love life. When we moved to my country 10 years later, it all reversed. I had to manage everything, or else my parents managed things for us. I taught her how to shop and cook. Even the house we rented had to stay the way it was with its eastern décor. My wife hated it. She began to withdraw more and more from me and eventually refused to sleep with me.*
>
> — R. from India

In many societies, a cultural or religious rule demands that either the man or the woman has the final say in most family matters. In northwestern Europe and in North America, the male and female partners usually share a more egalitarian (equal) power-balance.

If a husband comes from a country where men are expected to show strong masculinity (such as some Latin American and Mediterranean countries), and he marries someone whose concept of masculinity is caring and gentle (such as in Scandinavian countries), there will be conflicts in both marriage and parenting styles. His wife is longing for someone to cooperate with, but he might view cooperation as a threat to his masculinity. (See G. Hofstede's books for a fuller discussion on how these aspects influence relationships.)

TO THINK AND TALK ABOUT (23)

Who leads whom?

Currently, who leads in which aspect of your relationship and when? How might this change if you changed countries of residence?

86

What is your expectation of your partner's leadership role or of his/her response to your leadership?

What is his/her expectation of your leadership role or your response to his/her leadership?

---

5 Role expectations

Who does what and when?

Running a home involves some essential tasks. Who does what and when might change from the early years of the relationship until retirement, but even more so when the couple moves to another country. The children or possibly servants will do these tasks. Three of the main challenges that need to be kept in mind are:

- Behavior patterns prior to marriage might change after a couple marries and/or moves to one partner's country. One major surprise is when one partner suddenly expects his or her partner to assume an entirely different role than before.

- One partner's behavior might change when his or her parents arrive. Prior to a visit by his parents, for example, the husband might have helped in the kitchen, but now he expects his wife to do all of it; in his family, a man never enters the kitchen.

- One partner promises to change but doesn't.

"The woman you will marry isn't going to like how your mother still runs your life."

"That's easy. One day I will do what my mother says, and the next day I will do what her mother says."

The following is a common scenario of a male partner who comes from a male-dominant hierarchical culture and marries a woman who is an egalitarian;[4] they marry in her home country.

While in the country of his female partner during their courtship, he behaves as an egalitarian; that is, he shares equally in the household chores and has equal say in the decision-making process. Both partners work outside the home and share their income. He eats with her in the kitchen, he listens to her opinions with respect, and they submit to each other's requests and criticisms.

However, after they move back to his country, everything changes. Within a short time he conforms to the role that his society expects of him. He begins to "boss around" his wife, refrains from kitchen work, eats only with his male family members rather than with her, doesn't allow her to go out alone or to work outside the home, and manages all the money by himself. His wife is at first shocked, disappointed, and hurt.

She finally musters the courage to confront him. He explains to her his position in his family and his culture; but he then tells her that in his view, she is equally valuable. She responds with understanding but asks for compromises and flexibility. Together they find ways in which they can show respect for each other, both in private and in public, and without risking his family's disapproval. He shares a meal with his wife alone three evenings a week, and the rest of the week he eats with the men of the family.

---

[4] Here, an *egalitarian* is a *person* who is accustomed to equality of roles, power, and participation

Roles and routines: Who does what when?

Who is expected and allowed to work outside the home?
Who is supposed to do the "heavy lifting" (yard work, moving, repairs …)?
Who is expected to manage the household, clean, prepare the meals?
Who is expected to teach and to care for children?
Who manages the cash for food and household shopping?
Who is expected to earn the higher salary?
Who is to control the bank account, manage the savings and other property?
Who is expected to initiate love making?
Who decides to move the family to another location?
Who decides on interior décor and furnishings?

6   Managing finances

What do we do with my, your, and our money?

Studies show that the number-one area of conflict in a marriage or a union is *money.* How money is to be earned and spent, and by whom, and who manages it, are questions which every couple needs to ask. In an intercultural marriage, these issues can be more complex due to the differences in gender expectations. A change in the country of residence as well as the expectations of in-laws might also affect the way these questions are answered.

Chapter 3 lists the basic needs that all people have. How people try to meet these needs influences their use of money. While some might want to spend their extra money by going to the movies, others would rather send that money to their families back home. For those for whom security is important, depositing money into a savings account suffices, while for those who understand the risks, investing in stocks or real-estate seems wiser. If these variations lead to conflicts that cannot be resolved easily, a financial counselor or a seminar on household finances might be of help.

One source of confusion and disappointment is the variety of ways that bills are paid. The partner who comes from another country might not know at all how to follow the new country's procedures. Writing a check, obtaining and using a credit card, paying a bill with computerized teller machines or by computer, or keeping and balancing a budget — all these skills and customary practices vary from country to country. He or she will also need to learn how to transmit money in the correct currency to relatives. Ignorance in these matters can be costly.

In many Asian countries, parents support their children very generously during their schooling. But when these parents get old and are unable to support themselves, the children are expected to pay for their parents' well-being. In some European countries, the parents are legally responsible to pay for their children's education, their accommodation, and basic living needs until the children are twenty-seven years old, in some cases. And when parents become unable to support themselves adequately (or if there is not enough pension available), the grown children are legally required to provide for their care.

Whatever the culture combination, partners should compare carefully the rules and customs of paying bills, and discuss what is expected in regards to the financial care of family members.

TO THINK AND TALK ABOUT (25)

Money matters

How much (more) money do we need?
What material possessions do we want to acquire? How do we get them?
Why get rich or richer — to help others or to have more for ourselves?
Who might earn more and does it matter?
How much does each set of parents help when needed?
Do we owe our parents — how much and with interest or without?
Who manages the household money?
Who gets how much pocket money?
Do we want joint bank accounts or separate or both?
Investment and savings: Who, what, where and for how long?
What does "ours" include — his or her family and clan?
What happens if you inherit something from your parents — is it ours or yours?
What happens if I inherit something from my parents — is it ours or mine?
What happens to "ours" when one of us dies or leaves the marriage? Do the children automatically get the money, or does the spouse?

---

7   The next generation

What will shape their identity?

Children of an intercultural union are formed not only by the personalities and genes of their parents, but also by the societies and cultures they have lived in. As a result, they are more complex than others.

First, they have many advantages. Their parents can offer them the very great variety that exists between them through modeling and verbal training, through education, and through religious traditions. Children "pick up" the parts of their parents' identities which they are most comfortable with, adopt a unique combination of their parents' behavior and beliefs, and interpret them to their advantage.

Secondly, although they learn more than many other children and have richer lives in many ways, these children also suffer several *dis*advantages. For example, they might be subject to the pain of racism, ridicule, or rejection due to the difference in clothes, accent, customs, or religion. How children respond to these will affect their self-image. All this can be more painful if the parents do not resolve their cultural and personal conflicts, or if they do not *openly* respect each other. For it is primarily the parents who help their children form a positive image of their complex identity.

We always tell our children to mark down both Caucasian and Asian when they are asked which race they are, because they are both. And they are proud of it. I think it helps that we respect each other's cultural and racial identity in front of them.

— Dr. Heidi Chew

When growing up in New York City, I used to feel ashamed of my Chinese father, my Spanish mother and my mixed-race look. But as I got older, I learned to treasure the heritage I received from both. I majored in Spanish in college, and then studied medicine in Germany. While doing an internship in Canada, I met many Chinese there and began to learn Mandarin. I eventually worked as a medical doctor in a tribal village in Taiwan, which became my second home.

— Dr. Florence On

TO THINK AND TALK ABOUT (26)

Parenting and children

How many children do you wish to have? Gender? Names?
What do either partner's parents expect?
Will you use birth control? If so, which method?
Are you pro-life? Under what circumstances would you agree to an abortion, if any?
What religious ceremonies are to be performed in childhood? In adolescence?
Who will care for the children?
Who will discipline them? How?
Who chooses their schooling? Their careers?
What language will be spoken or taught?
Which religion will the children be exposed to and expected to follow?
How will you respond when the child does not conform to your hopes and expectations in regards to

- religious faith and practice?
- career ?
- marriage?
- place or future residence?

8 Dependence–Interdependence

What influence do our parents have?

Parents have a great influence on their offspring in the earlier years. These children gradually assume more responsibility as they grow older. Their dependency changes to independence. Eventually, as mentioned in section 9 of this chapter, it is the parents who become dependent on the adult children. These changes affect not only the adult children and their parents, but also the partners of the adult children.

One of the chief marriage-killers is when one partner has an *unhealthy* dependency, financial or emotional, on his parents or extended family. These parents or family elders might want to control some aspects of their child's life, such as which neighborhood the couple lives in, what toys the children may have, or what clothes are worn in public. If this is the case, partners need to take the time to talk with themselves, asking each other, "How shall we handle my (or your) parents when they try to interfere or control us?" and, "How can we continue to honor them and their needs, yet still protect our own relationship?"

Until recent decades, the Judeo-Christian tradition has been the basis for most Western marriages. It is understood from this tradition that when a young man or woman marries, he or she leaves the parents. (*"For this reason a man will leave his father and mother and be united to his wife...."* Genesis 2:24a, the Bible). What it means to leave one's parents varies from family to family. Even in Western cultures it certainly does not mean the husband or wife may neglect the parents when the parents are in need. On the contrary, in one of the Ten Commandments in the Judaic Law it also says, *"Honor your father and mother...."* (Exodus 20:12a; Deuteronomy 6:16a, the Bible). In the Gospels of Matthew and Mark, Jesus rebuked the Pharisees for using money for their temple instead of for the care of their elderly parents.

Conflicts and problems might result whenever this principle is interpreted differently among two partners. In some Asian cultures with the core values of Confucianism, Buddhism, and Hinduism, amongst others, the patriarch of the family (the oldest father) or in others the matriarch (the oldest mother), is expected to influence or even rule over matters of career, geography, and even the education of the grandchildren. In these cultures parents might threaten to withdraw their inheritance if their children do not follow their elders' suggestions.

In the case of a Western wife of a man from one of the above-mentioned cultures, a dilemma might arise. It might be that the parents of her husband might try to determine the role of the new wife even if she is a Westerner and has quite a different role expectation! She must then decide: Should she please her parents-in-law or herself? It is not always possible to know ahead of time the extent of the power her parents-in-law will have, or expect to have.

Her husband also has a dilemma. How willing is he to support his wife in the presence of his parents who oppose her? His wife might find it difficult to understand the pressure he feels from his parents and simultaneously from her. He needs her support as much as she needs his as they work through this together.

People, and especially partners, need each other, and yet, they don't need each other at the same time. Therefore, any family relationship is a balance between dependence, independence, and interdependence. A successful partnership balances all three to the satisfaction of both partners and their families. How can this be achieved? Certainly not by running away from it! Respect, patience, forgiveness, and lots of talking together are required to make such a partnership work.

TO THINK AND TALK ABOUT (27)

Family influence and extended family issues

In what ways and to what degree are you and/or your partner dependent on your or his/her parents or extended family ...

- financially? (loans, inheritance, day-to-day support)
- materially? (housing, car, food)
- career-wise? (job connections, family business)
- emotionally?

How powerful is the influence of my/your parents in our joint decision-making?
Are any of our siblings dependent on either of us?
Who will care for our elderly parent(s) when in need?
How do we, should we, handle conflict with either of our parents?
What expectations have each of our parents, grandparents, or siblings of me? Of my partner?

9 Responsibilities beyond "just us"

How do we honor our extended families?

In contrast to the more individualistic societies of the West, people who originate in other parts of the world often value the extended family, especially the parents and the siblings, and this value does not change when a young person marries. In fact, he or she is often expected to assume responsibility for those in the extended family who are in need.

Honoring the parents

Many cultural groups place a high value on honoring the parents. This means different things in different cultures. To honor a parent or family member is not just a speech or an action, but also an attitude. The goal is to meet a need (or fulfill a wish, in some cases) of the parent whenever or however possible. In some cases, a married couple might live with one of the sets of parents in order to fulfill the honor required. Or, honoring them might mean having the parents of one of the partners live with the couple in their home, not necessarily out of financial need, but because they feel they belong there and want to contribute to the relational community of this family. In some groups, honoring extended family members, such as grandparents, aunts, uncles, or older siblings, is also very important.

Elderly parents

Sometimes the eldest or the youngest is responsible to care for and provide for the elderly parents when they become physically and/or financially dependent. Placing elderly parents into institutional care is unthinkable in many non-Western countries. When one refuses to pay respect to the partner's parents in this manner, that partner usually suffers.

Siblings

Brothers and sisters often follow each other to a Western or wealthier country and expect to live with the one who has arrived there first. This live-in situation might hold for an extended amount of time, especially if the established sibling is married and has a home. For example, shortly after an American woman married an Iranian, she was shocked to find that her husband had invited three of his younger brothers to come to the USA to live with them. In many non-Western cultures, even young men in their late teens or twenties are often expected to provide for their younger or less fortunate siblings, especially when the parents are no longer able to.

The different ways of interpreting and applying the principle of honoring the parents or family can cause great conflict for a couple. It is important that these issues are discussed and resolved long before they come up!

Chapter 5   Creating at the Canvas

How shall we proceed?

The artwork can begin! The partners are paired, you've settled on a studio, you've merged the materials, devised the design — but now you want to know how to proceed creating your artwork together, right?

By observing many intercultural couples throughout the years whose relationship showed signs of becoming a masterpiece, the authors have gleaned the following tips:

I   Know your colors

The seven visuals in this book are in various shades of gray. When presented in different colors (see cover), they come to life and light in a new way.

In an intercultural relationship, there will always be at least two cultural colors. Do you know your own? The following questions are those that each partner must ask for him-or herself.

- Do I know who I am, what I like, choose, or value; and what I do not like, choose, or value? (Refer back to Chapter 3.)

- Do I know who my partner is, what he or she likes, chooses, or values; and what he doesn't like, choose, or value?

For two partners to work together, they need to know their own canvas, colors, brushes, and palette, plus the ones of their partner. Only then are they able to decide what to do with their own, and with those of their partner.

If you are not aware of your own cultural identity, you may end up giving up things that might turn out later to be very important to you. You may eventually miss them; and when you do, you will realize how important they were to you. And it will be hard to get them back.

Before I came to my husband's country, I knew what was

important to me. I saw how hard it was for the other foreign wives to become themselves again. Even though I knew my husband didn't always agree with my approach to life here, I always made sure that he knew that I loved him.

– J. from Cyprus

2   Allow for diversity

Artists can only paint with the colors they each have. What the artists do with them, how they combine them, and how they use them to create a whole new painting, for example, is up to them. There will be times when one partner prefers to use his or her own colors rather than those of the other.

One partner cannot expect the other to adapt to a new culture so completely as to be identical with it. This would be unrealistic and unloving. Rather, differences between the partners are healthy. They should be tolerated and even welcomed. Differences can be *enhancements*; that is, they can help partners to be better individuals and to become a more exciting couple.

Therefore, celebrate those differences! Write down some of them, and smile. Could it be that these differences attracted you to this person in the first place?

> *I think it's counterproductive to insist on what is important only to me. Instead, I look at my wife's list of tastes, beliefs, preferences, values, and behaviors, and say to myself, "I don't like some of those things," but I still choose to accept her. The less I try to change her, the easier it is to live with these differences and still find ways to be happy.*
>
> *-M. from Lebanon*

> *I used to feel as though I was going insane because my husband watched football every Saturday and Monday on television. It was the noise that bothered me the most! I finally got him earphones for the TV so I don't have to hear it. Now he's happy, and I'm happy. And on other days we watch the news and other shows together.*
>
> *-S. from Slovenia*

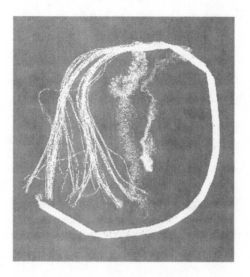

A ribbon unravelling

Ribbons are used for decoration for beauty. They are accessories on gift packages or the trim on dresses.

A ribbon could unravel. If it does, the marvellously fine threads and gossamer edging reveal themselves. Pull too hard, though, and the ribbon would be lost altogether.

The process of adjustment is similar to unravelling. Only you can know when enough is enough, when to fix the ends and set your limits.

But those free ends — maybe they would be useful in some way; they are still attached to the ribbon!!

Take care of yourself and of each other.

As intercultural partners, your goals should include:

- to be aware of what influences, cultural preferences, tastes, and mannerisms make up who you are (see Chapter 3);

- to be able to tolerate, accept, or enjoy diversity (different ways of seeing and doing things), and respect the dignity and worth of others who are different;

- to be willing to lay aside, sacrifice, and negotiate some preferences and expectations for the sake of harmony with your partner (see Chapter 3), while finding ways to keep your own unique identity.

3   Be ready to change

Making some changes will not destroy your identity, but it might unravel it a bit, or it might reshape it a little — sometimes temporarily, sometimes permanently. Some changes are necessary to make a union of diverse partners work. You might find that you have to make some difficult and long-term decisions about who you are and what aspects of your identity you want to keep. Before you decide to partner together for life, it is therefore good to ask yourself:

- How much am I prepared to sacrifice or give up of my own culture in the relationship?

- How much of my partner's culture do I choose to tolerate, accept, or adjust to?

This should not be a power struggle, but a voluntary dance, in which there is both freedom and cooperation. While each partner's steps can move in opposite and differing directions, there can still be togetherness. Of course, there will be two sets of dance steps to learn.

One example of willing adaptation is a widow named Ruth, an ancestor of Jesus of Nazareth. After her foreign husband died, she said something to her mother-in-law, which a bride and groom still recite to each other at wedding ceremonies today:

> *Where you go I will go, and where you stay, I will stay. Your people shall be my people and your God my God. Where you die I will die, and there will I be buried.*
> *— Ruth 1:16,17. The Bible*

And she did exactly that. She went to the country of her mother-in-law and married again.

> *As an American, my husband found it difficult to get accustomed to my large extended family with its strong family ties. Whenever he was with my family, which enjoys lots of laughter and closeness, he felt lonely and neglected by me. He says he actually hated me during that time and came away totally depressed. I was finally able to realize that what he actually missed was that intimate closeness to me. He told me so. After that, I made sure I found times to be with him alone on our holidays, and then found other times to be with my whole family without him there.*
>
> *-A. from Greece*

Adapting to someone does not mean giving up one's entire identity. Identity develops. It is never fixed nor permanent. As time goes on, you will let go of some influences from childhood, you will learn to treasure others even more, and you will adopt new ideas, tastes, and behaviors. Some of these changes occur automatically and without your awareness. Other changes will be conscious and deliberate. Simply be ready for changes!

It should also be noted that as people age, their minds revert back to their earlier years, even to the point of talking more in their childhood language. This can surprise their partners and children, especially if they cannot understand that language.

Just as the watercolor paper has a color wash laid on it that tints the picture permanently, your underlying culture will never completely vanish. In other words, you will never be able to change some of these culturally learned values and behaviors. However, until you become aware of your own cultural colors, you cannot lay them aside nor integrate those of your partner. And that will mean dissatisfaction, frustration, tension, and alienation in your relationship. So you need to become aware of what these cultural colors are.

4 Find some unifying factors

Is there a common set of tastes, traditions, beliefs, priorities, or behaviors that you share together or that are compatible with each other? Think back to the time when you first met: What attracted you to each other? What situation drew you together? Reminisce together, and if possible, repeat them! Enjoy them as often as possible. Celebrate what you do have together, including the memories of the past.

TO THINK AND TALK ABOUT (28)

Things we enjoy doing together

Make a list of the things you and your partner enjoy doing together. Include goals, projects, people, activities, fun things, or work, and go out and celebrate doing them.
Refer to Appendix II "Personal Priorities of Choice."

5   Make a love-for-life commitment

True love means commitment. When a couple is committed to maintaining the relationship and to restoring it when it has gone sour, the partnership has a better chance of survival. This commitment builds mutual trust in one another and a feeling of security. It says, "We really do value, cherish, and love each other." That's not just a warm, fuzzy feeling, but the *decision* to serve you *both*, not merely yourself. It is not the same as lazy resignation. It allows for times of anger and frustration, which are natural feelings that give rise to honest communication and problem-solving. When one partner angers the other, or when there is miscommunication or other disappointments, commitment means a *decision* to talk about the pain and its cause, and to listen to each other until a solution is found.

Commitment enables partners to find ways of creating for yourself the happiness and intimacy you long for with your partner, regardless how long it takes and how difficult that search may be. Of course, it could be that for at least one of you, the top priority is not happiness at all, but responsible social relationships. In either case, a mutual commitment would boost the ability to listen to your partner, endure a little more, be patient and, most importantly, give the relationship another chance again and again.

> *Whenever I start to feel I married the wrong person, I take some time to grieve my choice and list all the positives of the relationship. Then I feel better, behave better, and my partner notices the difference and smiles at me again.*
>
> *— M. from Ireland*

> *Sometimes I feel sorry for myself because I was blind and stupid back then. And then I feel just too tired or lazy to do anything about it. When I'm like that, what helps me is to begin the new*

day with the resolve to start fresh, to love, to forgive, and to give.
If I don't feel like it today, I hope I feel like it again tomorrow or
the day after tomorrow.

— *A. from Brazil*

6   Draw from a higher (spiritual) source

Even when we do our best to remain true to our commitment to one another, we humans fail. We are so preoccupied with meeting our needs for food, shelter, security, significance, belonging, and peace, that we often ignore the needs and wants of others. Yet we feel disappointed and frustrated when others don't give us what we want or need!

If we do not know how to deal wisely with these natural feelings of disappointment or frustration, we might allow greed, hatred, or revenge to steer our behavior. The possible result? Violence and even murder. Neither the best government law enforcement in the world, nor all the good advice from books, even such as this one, will ever fully resolve this dilemma.

To attempt to resolve this dilemma, adherents of religions say that it is their faith, its teachings, and its rituals that give them personal wisdom and strength to maintain an orderly, peaceful relationship with other people. To name a few examples, Buddha taught people to empathize with the sufferings of others and develop the mind-set of equanimity in all things; some Hindu traditions promote loyalty as an aspect of love; the Islamic tradition encourages orderly respect and love within the definite boundaries of the broader family; and the Jewish scriptures promote loving one's neighbor as oneself. Jesus of Nazareth underscored the Jewish teaching but added that anyone who is put in our path could be our neighbor, and that we should be kind to our enemies and not seek revenge.

Why is it so difficult for people to follow these ideals, especially the rules to love others and to be kind to an enemy? How can we obey this rule at all? Christians teach that when we ignored the rules of our Creator-God, our relationship with him was severed, and our ability to healthily relate to one another was greatly weakened. However, God cared for us so much that he himself provided a way for us to reconnect with him and with each other: God came to Earth in human form (as the baby who was named Jesus), taught and healed many, and then willingly allowed himself to be cruelly sacrificed on a Roman cross. Through this death, Jesus paid for our rebellion called *sin*. And then, three days later, Jesus came back to life. His followers believe that when we confess our sin to God and thank him for his sacrifice, he will forgive us and empower us to love others in the same way as he loved us. That empowerment, they teach, is the key to loving relationships and to forgiveness.

7 Be ready to forgive

Forgiving someone is not natural. Counter-attack and revenge, or withdrawal and escape are more natural. These feelings are meant to give us the energy to protect ourselves, but if we hold on to them too long, they make us weak. There is a healthier way, and that is, to forgive each other.

This is easier said than done.

If your partner admits hurting you and asks you for forgiveness, your forgiveness means, "You owe me nothing. I will erase your debt. I will not count it against you any more." Of course, saying that doesn't necessarily make you feel warm and fuzzy! The following are important things to remember:

- Forgiveness is not the same as forgetting. Unfortunately human brains, when healthy, can't forget, especially not those events that hurt you emotionally.

- Forgiveness is not a feeling but a choice. It can take years before the feelings of hurt and anger completely subside. Over time, they will become less painful, but occasionally will "flare up" when something reminds you of the offense. When that happens, you must remember again that you chose forgiveness.

- Forgiveness is a decision to let go all desires and plans for any kind of payback.

- Forgiveness is never an excuse or license for your offender to willfully repeat the offense. If the repeated offense harms you, you can forgive, but you should also protect yourself from further harm.

- Forgiveness does not mean that you may protect a criminal from due justice. The law should be on your side to protect you and others from further harm.

- Forgiveness in its truest form releases bitterness and frees us to love again.

To forgive is not always easy. When it seems too hard, it might help to remember the times when you were forgiven. Then decide to *be willing* to forgive. Finally, ask God to enable you to forgive others as he has forgiven you.

8 Encourage each other

One of the questions you need to ask each other is, "How do you want me to say or show you that I love you?"

In some cultures, the husband might consider the woman's work in the house as "an act of love," and she does it gladly as her way of expressing her love for him. "I write him notes of appreciation by e-mail," says one wife. "And I show that I love her by providing her with a house and a car," answers her husband.

Unfortunately, many times these "acts of love" are not recognized as messages of love. They are either taken for granted or overlooked because they are not the language of love that is understood by the receiver!

The solution sounds easier than it is. "Treating others as you would have others treat you" is hard enough. Doing something different, or better or more, for your partner than what you hope your partner would do for you — that's even harder. One way to learn is to ask your partner several times, "What would you like me to do for you now?" Or, "Is it Okay if I …?" Or, "Would you like me to …?" Until you know your partner very well, don't take for granted that you know! If you ask, don't assume your partner will tell you or even knows what to tell you. But don't give up asking!

> *My husband is not a talker, but I've learned to recognize and appreciate his love language. His is touch. Each time he embraces me, it's as if he says, "Hey, I choose to love you still, despite everything in the past and present. And I hope you accept me as I am, despite everything in the past and present." And when I see it that way, I celebrate.*
>
> *— C. from Canada*

9 Make your needs known

Let your partner know what you need and want in a way that he "hears" and understands; likewise, find out what your partner needs and wants from you. How you do this should partially depend on the culture of your partner. You need to find out what timing, voice, and choice of words will work best, so that your partner will hear you and consider what you say. Words, deeds, a show of emotions, or shouting and whining, or a simple note on the refrigerator might be more effective in some cultures. Silence and a special way of eye contact, however, might work better in others.

Many Westerners don't have the ability to perceive what needs their partners have or which things bother them. Rather, they expect their partners to tell them verbally. This might be different in another culture where the young are trained to notice the needs of another, and to understand what silence or body language communicates.

If your partner is a European or North American, it would be good to learn to state your wishes in a matter-of-fact but polite manner. After you have expressed them, you can leave the response to your partner. If your partner promises something, but forgets, you can repeat your request in a calm, neutral tone.

If you find it easy to state what you need or want and you have a non-Western partner who finds it much more difficult to state what he or she needs or wants, you may need to ask some questions. But even if you ask your partner gently, you may not get the "real" reply. You might still need to observe how your partner interacts with friends and family before you can *really* understand what he or she says and when.

"Loss of face" and its counterpart, "saving face," are complicated social sensitivities which are very important to many, especially to Asians. It may affect not only how one's wishes or complaints are expressed, but how the partner receives those messages. If you live outside of the West, you might need to be even more aware of this.

You might discover that your partner wishes you to be more sensitive to his needs so that he doesn't need to tell you what they are. Of course, with time you can learn to recognize his nonverbal cues, but you must still be careful not to misinterpret them. With the passage of time, it can be hoped that the partner will talk more, and, in turn, that *you* will improve in the area of sensitivity.

I always raised my voice when asking my husband to do something for me. Then he became quieter and it seemed as if he ignored or avoided me. When we finally talked about it, he told me that my angry or loud voice reminded him of his father, and it automatically made him lose face, or feel ashamed.

— N. from Indonesia

One reason that our relationship has worked is that we communicate well with each other, despite the fact that our mother tongues are different from one another. We always ask each other, "Did I understand you correctly?" and then we repeat what the other has said. This helps clarify whether we've really understood each other. You might say that we as a bi-cultural couple have an edge over mono-cultural couples who don't do this.

— F. from North America

If you are verbal, direct, or emotionally expressive in stating your needs, your partner might be shocked or offended. Ask how you can express yourself so that your partner hears you.

Always check verbally to see if you understood.
Talk about your inability to "read" your partner's cues,
and ask him or her for help.

If none of the above works, it might be wise to consider lowering your expectations. If your expressed need is important to you, then consider having it met in a different way that is appropriate within your moral and cultural boundaries.

10 Confront your partner for your partner's and your own sakes

If your partner does something that may be dangerous to the health or well-being of either of you, don't wait for a crisis to say something. Possible examples include abuse of stimulants, drugs, or alcohol; walking alone at night; obsessive gambling or Internet use. Choosing the wisest time to confront is important. Talking about these concerns just before bedtime or during a meal might make things worse! Ask your partner, "When and where is a good time for us to talk?" and hold her to the time and place you agree on, if you can. If you are afraid of your partner's reaction, find a third person you both trust, and talk about it together.

11 Don't panic when your partner criticizes you

Your partner claims you used the paint brush the wrong way again, and the picture is now spoiled! Does it mean you should toss the painting in the trash, or worse, give up on the partnership and give up everything you have worked on so far? Maybe there are some other options:

- If you agree that the cause of the criticism was truly a mistake, whether intended or not intended, thank the partner for noticing it, and apologize.

- If possible, take responsibility for the consequences of your mistake.

- Try to change your habit or pattern that causes a problem.

- If you believe you did nothing wrong but that your partner misunderstood, or if you have a different opinion, say so, but do so politely and matter-of-factly. Maintaining your composure is more productive than becoming defensive!

12 Handle conflict creatively

Don't shy away from conflict! It is normal, and it is to be expected, especially in an intercultural relationship. When differences are discussed with respect and with an open mind, conflicts can strengthen a relationship. Lots of open, honest, and respectful conversations over your differences can be very rewarding. The goal should not be to convince the other to change. Instead, it should be to gain understanding of the other's viewpoint. Pushing the conflicts under the rug, called "peace at all cost," usually makes things worse.

The ways people resolve conflicts
vary from culture to culture and family to family;
The differences may become a conflict in itself.

In some cultures, the woman is always expected to yield to, or give in to, the opinion of her spouse. In others, it is the final word of the most senior parent, male or female, that reigns supreme. In still others, a neutral mediator is called in to help. Some couples try to resolve the conflict with sex — putting the conflict temporarily "on hold." Others shout at each other until they get tired, then come back to resume the topic when they have cooled off. A consensus, a compromise, or a synthesis of the two opposing opinions would be three possible ways to end the conflict.

It helps to remember that things are never really what they seem. Underneath most arguments, there are layers of hidden, unspoken cultural values, beliefs, and experiences that influence what a person wishes, thinks, or asserts. One of these layers could also be a distorted sense of reality, such as from a trauma in the past, from the intake of alcohol or drugs, or from a psychosis or a physical ailment. Awareness and understanding of these layers is a good beginning.

> *In some ways, I think we are better off than our friends who have married within their own culture. At least we expect conflicts and aren't afraid to say we don't understand.*
>
> *— M. from Spain*

Before another conflict

- Discuss the different ways you resolve conflicts in your cultural upbringing during a peaceful time together.

- Try to remember some conflicts you already resolved together, and ask, "How did we resolve the conflict? Can we repeat what worked?"

- Think back on a conflict that took a long time to resolve (or maybe did not get resolved). Ask, "What did we try that didn't work? Can we let go of what didn't work?"

During a conflict

- Ask the *why* questions: "What drives you and me to think the way we do, and why is this so important to me? And why is it so important to you?"

- Explore the reason for the reason. Ask, "What cultural insights might be helpful in finding the cause?"

- Be prepared to re-evaluate the cultural value or belief at the base of this conflict, adjust it, or temporarily set it aside if a compromise is needed.

- Try to do what worked in previous conflicts.

- Ask each other, "What can we agree on for now?"

Angelina, a Brazilian woman, and her Finnish husband were visiting her parents in Brazil. When her parents wanted to look after the children, her husband insisted that it was his job to do so; no one outside the family should take that responsibility.

"Here in Brazil," she said in defense of her parents, "it is not common for a man to watch the children; it is more normal for the grandparents to look after them. Besides, they want to see the children more often. And the kids love their grandparents!" She felt angry at her husband for upsetting her parents.

Yet having lived in Finland, she understood his side, too. She then proposed a compromise. The grandparents would spend time with the children while the couple visited friends together; then the husband would take care of the children while the wife spent time with her parents.

Remember, this is an artwork you are creating together. Ask yourselves, "Is there room for compromise?" When and how often do you give in to your partner's perspective, and how often does he or she see yours? Perhaps you need to dare to defend your position, or you need to brainstorm new ideas until you agree.

3 massive thunderclaps with lightening changed the whole mood & visibility in the valley —

Reflection contributes to creativity

These images came from a holiday in Adelboden, Switzerland. The changes in mood and light of that same fixed mountain scene are so dramatic! The stylized ones with the sharp distinctions of light and dark of early morning, painted in whites and gray, were in sharp contrast to the stormy scenes with their rapidly changing mists, hiding the certainties underneath.

Observations of change recorded in a sketch book are an essential source of ideas in the creative process. As a gift for a young Swiss-Mexican couple, the top sketch of alpine rocks and snows was painted in Mexican colors: peaches, lime greens, and oranges. This combination of rock and color symbolized their union almost perfectly.

**Allow your cultural differences to add vitality.
If some things don't work, reflect and start again.
You'll be surprised at what you can give and receive.**

13 Loosen up

When was the last time you laughed — really laughed? If you feel that you've lost your sense of humor, that is, you find it difficult to laugh with others or at yourself, it's time to have a look at why, and do something about it.

In the beginning years, living with someone from another culture *will often be* culture shock. Adjustment to a partner who is different from you, or adjusting to a new culture, or adjustment to your partner who changes in your culture — all these adjustments are hard work, and they sometimes get more difficult as time goes on. In short, an intercultural relationship is often stressful, even more so than many other partnerships. And too much stress can take its toll on the body, the mind, and on the emotional well-being.

There could be many other reasons for your stress: unresolved conflicts from the past, or stress in your firm or job, for example. Talking with others you can trust might shed light on the things that trouble you. Changing your thinking and behavior might reduce some of your stress. If you have trouble falling asleep at night, or if you feel like sleeping too much, or if you have no appetite, or if you begin to have negative, self-destructive ideas, talking with a medical doctor is a must. Physical activity, hobbies, music, short vacations, good nourishment, interaction with supportive friends, a different outlook towards the stressors of life — all these can help restore your energy, your zest for life, and your ability to laugh. When they do, you will be easier to live with.

While the stress factor can affect your relationship with your partner, your relationship can also be an avenue for relief.

- Find ways in which you can vent your feelings without hurting your partner's feelings.

- Stop the blame-game (yourself and others) and accept your and your partner's limitations.

- Take a break from complaining and count your blessings.

- Live a lot, laugh a lot, love a lot!

14 Draw from positive memories

Your positive memories can serve to help you as you look for solutions and for ways that make your relationship happier. Occasionally it may seem that the feelings of warmth and love you felt for one another when you began the relationship are gone. When that happens, think back and remember how it all started, and ask yourself,

- What was there about my partner that attracted me?

- What did we do together when we first met that made us happy and harmonious?

- What did I do, think, or believe in the past that helped me respond to difficult situations in a constructive, helpful way?

- What good things have I received or experienced that I can be grateful for?

15 Deal with negative memories that impact your present thoughts and feelings

When your partner does or says something that bothers or angers you, and you respond emotionally, it is rarely just that *one* thing that has triggered your reaction. You are re-playing a pattern from your childhood. When you identify that memory of the past and talk to someone about it, you will find it easier to separate your current feelings from those in the past and to respond more appropriately to the present situation. This is a process that involves time and patience.

Negative memories can also accumulate within the partnership. When there is a build-up of frustration about something in your partner's culture, you might grow increasingly angry toward him or her, even though your partner did nothing to cause it. Take some time out and reflect. Ask yourself why you are so angry. If you can't figure it out, talk about your feelings and confusion with your partner or with someone you can trust.

16 Acknowledge your limitations and get expert help

A successful relationship is never automatic. The goals, dreams, and hopes you each have for the relationship might differ. You are both human, and that means that you both have limitations. It is not natural for you to love someone who disappoints you, to forgive someone who has hurt you, to endure someone who doesn't change, and to sacrifice some cultural preferences for your partner. It is even less natural to remain committed to a person who is so different, or so difficult. Just look at the divorce rate in countries where it is allowed and easy to get!

Yet in a recent survey, 85% of adults in the USA claimed that they wanted a partner for life. So what is the solution? When you have car trouble, you go to a mechanic who knows more about cars than you do. When you have a toothache, you go to a dentist for help. So why not go to a "marriage doctor" when your relationship is in trouble and when nothing you have tried so far has made it better?

If you feel that you are not "mature" enough as described in Chapter 1 Section 12, or you carry some painful scars from the past that interfere with your current relationship, or you have difficulty resolving conflicts with your partner, or you find it too challenging to recognize all the cultural aspects of your partner, then talk to a trusted friend, family member, or mentor — particularly someone who understands the cultural differences between you and your partner.

17 Talk about children before you have them

The arrival of children can bring joy to the parents and renewed attention from both sets of grandparents. Accompanying this excitement of the first baby's arrival are often major arguments and conflicts. Before you even plan to have children, ask each other a few questions and make a compromise for each of the following:

- What are some rituals important to you when a child is born or soon afterward? Why and when do you do them?

- What are some taboos?

- Who will take responsibility for the material welfare of the child?

- Whose mother or parents will come to visit and when? How much authority will they have in the rearing or care of the child?

- Which culture, religion, or practices do you want to influence the child the most?

> *We hope that our example as a family of diversity and oneness inspires others in our town to get along with each other. We teach our children to tolerate and respect one another and to learn from each other, mostly by doing so ourselves and by showing them how it's done. We hope that as a result there will eventually be less prejudice and racial hatred around us.*
> *— H. from Germany*

18 Ready, get set, go!

If you and your partner can say "yes" to each of the following, you are perhaps ready to begin a long-term commitment to each other.

- We have observed each other in varied situations over a period of at least six months, and we still accept, respect, trust, and cherish each other for what we are, without hoping that the other will change.

- We can imagine living with each other even if our current circumstance, geographic location, career and/or lifestyle were to change in the future.

- We are more happy to be with each other than without; that is, we experience our relationship as mutually beneficial, healthy, safe and pleasurable — at least more so than not.

- We each choose to stay with each other, with the determination to creatively make our relationship work and last, even though it is possible to live independently of each other.

- Should we have children, we are able not only to provide shelter and food for them, but also give them a loving, supportive, united, and emotionally secure atmosphere.

Appreciation of any work of art is in the eyes of the beholders. If the observer is looking for either fine lines and exact representation, or dramatic color and expression of feeling or comic reflection, he or she will measure any work of art accordingly. A work with fine lines and exact representation will be considered excellent by one observer, but not by another. In a similar way, a relationship will be judged by observers according to their own expectations.

In the end, however, it is you, the partners, whose satisfaction or dissatisfaction really matters. If you are satisfied, then the relationship can be considered a successful one.

On Display — An Interplay

How shall we impact the world?
The world is watching, waiting
to see the end result
of what we create together:

a series of life projects,
some of which
may never be quite finished.

As we work together,
the two of us become
an art piece ourselves —
a model of intercultural harmony.

This is a higher cause.
It helps us to survive
and to master
our work of art.

And as we do,
we pass on hope —
hope to the larger world.

To Think And Talk About

We strongly recommend that you do not attempt to look at, or discuss, all of the following questions at one sitting, but rather only one or two sections at a time.

(1) Stereotypes

After you list your generalizations and stereotypes of your partner's culture, then ask your partner, "Is this true of you? Is this true of your family? Is this mostly true of your culture, or country? How are you similar to your own people? How is your partner similar to his or hers?"

(2) Expressions of feelings for one another

Which expressions of feelings of love or affection would you like to receive from your partner? *Compare your list with that of your partner.*

    eye contact, smiling eyes, smiling mouth
    touch, massage
    words, pet name, being listened to,
    music
    gifts
    praise, endearing words, love letters, poems
    being nearby, working at home
    cleaning, cooking for me
    taking me out to eat or for a walk
    other ways?
Talk about which are hard for you to receive or do, and why.

(3) Boundaries of Sexual Expression

What are the social rules of my family, society, religious leaders and the laws of my country in regards to sexual behavior before marriage? During marriage?

How are these rules different from those of my partner's parents, country or society?

How are they different in the country where I presently live?

How are they different in the country where we plan to live?

What are my boundaries? What are his or hers?

(4) Family acceptance

Do my parents accept my partner?

Do my siblings, grandparents, cousins, etc.?

Does my community or society accept my partner?

If the answer is no to the above, how does my partner react?

Do his or her parents accept me?

If do not, how do they behave? How do I react?

Do the siblings, grandparents, cousins, etc. accept me?

If not, how do they show it? How do I react?

Will they (or do they) accept our children?

(5) Communication styles

Observe your families and each other's families. Which of the following behaviors are commonly practiced in your and your partner's families?

Direct – Verbal
   verbal expression of wants or needs; tone, choice of words
   use of actual name or terms of endearment
   honest and direct expressions of feelings, ideas, thoughts
   flattery, compliments, praise
   strong language: curse words or abuse of sexual terms, name calling
   refusal or disagreement: (how?)
   linear, to the point
   brief, simple

Indirect – (Verbal or non-verbal)
   silence; use of pauses
   gestures with hands, fingers, body posture
   frown, tears, mouth hanging
   head shaking, hanging, nodding side-ways, up and down
   tone of voice (expressing emotions)
   soft voice, loud voice
   sarcasm; teasing (either as indirect anger or as endearment)

Other styles
   monologue: speaking without waiting for response
   dialogue: speaking briefly and expecting a response
   interrupting or overlapping
   flowery language: hyperboles and exaggerations
   defensive, argumentative for sake of control
   circular, emphasis on context

Tell each other what you like about the other's style of communication. Then talk about what you wish the partner do differently

(6) Maturity

Am I becoming more and more able to ...
  consciously accept or reject the beliefs, preferences and behaviors of persons in my upbringing?
  respect other people's ways of seeing and doing things, when possible?
  be open to the advice and perspective of others?
  respond to the needs of others, not out of a need to be loved, but simply for the ultimate welfare of others?
  forgive the wrong of others, yet find legal ways to protect myself from repeated injustice?
  be honest in the relationship that is important to me?
  be loyal and committed even when it isn't easy?
  carry out expected responsibilities?
  be willing to lay aside some preferences, yet find ways to keep my own unique identity?
  maintain a sense of humor and enjoy the present?
In my culture, what qualities would be found in a mature person? Am I considered mature enough to partner with someone who is culturally different? Is my partner?

(7) Choosing where to live — your country or mine?

The foreign partner should ask the other ...
If I should move back to my country some day, would you want to move there with me? Why or why not?
How would our relationship change or develop?
What would you like? What would you miss?
Would you mind being taught by me? (Language, customs, rules) Would you be allowed to work there, considering visa regulations, the degree of education, career/job experience and training?
Would my country be good for our children? Why or why not, and in what respects?
Is there another country where we could both live?
Where will you want to retire — in your country or in mine or in-?
Is it possible for you to become a citizen of my country?
If you met in your own country, ask your partner to ask you the same.

(8) Laws of the land

Exchange information about varying laws in your respective countries, and research corresponding laws about the following in the country where you live or expect to live:

the right to work
proof of identity
immigration, citizenship
right to vote
visa and passport
marriage registration
child discipline
financial care of parents
permission to purchase land
physical assault
sexual assault
marriage rites, laws
divorce
discipline of children
freedom of religion
religious expression
religious conversion
bribes or fraud
dress, hair or make-up
care of elderly parents
traffic and driving regulations
noise, curfews

(9) Cultural Identity Issues

Which of my identity (tastes, beliefs, or practices) do I want my partner to adopt?
What parts of my partner's identity am I willing to accept or adopt?
What parts of my identity does my partner want me to give up or change?
What parts of my partner's identity do I want him/her to change?
What cultural parts of me do I revert to for comfort when I'm sad, angry or frustrated?

(10) My upbringing and family of origin

What am I proud of when I think of my ethnic origin?
What am I proud of when I think of my family heritage?
What events shaped or influenced my grandparents and my parents? How

did these circumstances or events affect them? How did these circumstances affect me?

What were some of their basic values, beliefs and views that influenced me? (Include moral laws, values, superstitions, mottos, world view, principles, views about the opposite sex, etc.)

What superstitions, mottos, attitudes do I have about the opposite sex?
How did my parents discipline me and show me love?
How is my relationship with them now?
What place or role do I have among my siblings?
What am I most thankful for when I think of my upbringing?
What am I ashamed, sad or angry about when I think of my family of origin?

(11) Basic Needs

Rearrange the list of basic needs in the column below according to what you think is most important to your current circumstances.
security (physical survival, nourishment, shelter, safety)
significance (feeling worthwhile, having a role in society)
love & belonging (loved by and loving family and friends)
freedom (independence, autonomy, privacy
pleasure (fun, beauty, sensual pleasure, and enjoyment)
Which three needs are currently the most important to me?
How do we differ in the way we meet these needs?

(12) Interests, tastes, hobbies, pastime

Interests, tastes, hobbies, pastime — Name yours.
sport — active, passive, what kind?
music to listen to — active, passive, what kinds?
dance — what kind?
music performed — how, with whom, what kind?
movies — what type?
books — what type and how often?
television programs — what type, when, how often or how long?
visual beauty — what interior décor, architecture, flowers, colors?
fashion — what clothes, hairstyles, colors?
food — what kind? Cook yourself or eat out?
What about other interests, fascinations, tastes, passions?
What could we do together that we both enjoy?
What will you do with me that you don't enjoy?

What would I do with you that I don't enjoy?

What would or could I do alone? How would or does that affect our relationship?

(13) Social Rules and Manners

What was customary or allowed in your home or social group?

What do you find offensive in the culture of your partner?

How would you want your partner to behave when your family comes to visit?

How would my partner want me to behave when his/her family comes to visit?

How are the following different in my partner's culture?

space between speakers

meeting strangers: how? when? where?

greeting friends or relatives the same sex; of the opposite sex: how?

body posture in front of elders or superiors

show of affection to partner in public

introducing friends to your partner or visa versa

friendliness: to whom and when?

eye contact: who looks at whom and when?

sitting or getting up or standing when?

legs and feet position; hand gestures

table manners: touching food when with which hand or utensils?

spitting, belching, coughing, and sneezing in public

gifts and gift giving, to whom, what, on which occasion?

other taboos: (things not allowed to do in public)

(14) Hospitality

Exchange the customs you grew up with and compare with those that are acceptable in the country where you now live (or will live).

Hosting

Who do you like to host? When, how often and how long?

Do you invite people or do you hope they come uninvited?

What do you serve when?

Do you just bring something or ask first?

Do you offer food, and how often, after the guest says "No, thank you?"

Do men and women sit and eat together when guests are present?

Where do the children eat?

What do you expect your guests to bring when you invite them to a meal? If nothing, why?

Being a guest:
> Can I come only when invited? Without prior notice?
> Should I come at the exact time the host said I should come?
> Or am I expected later, and if so, how much later?
> What do I bring to the host when invited? Should I ask?
> Do I take off my shoes before entering the main part of the home?
> Do I help myself to the food on the table or wait until it is offered?
> How do I use a knife and fork in your country? Or do I at all?
> Is burping forbidden, taboo, or encouraged?
> What about slurping soup? Blowing my nose? Or …?
> Must I say "no" when offered something, even if I really want it? How many times should I refuse?
> Am I allowed in the kitchen?
> How do I show appreciation afterward?

(15) Rituals and holiday traditions

Compare some traditions or rituals that each of you wishes to continue while in this relationship, and state specifically how you like to observe them.
> holiday celebrations (Which ones? What do you want to continue to observe even if you live in another country?)
> morning, noon and evening rituals
> days off from work or weekends
> birthdays, anniversaries (How celebrated? What do you expect from your partner?)
> birth rites, coming-of-age rites, death of a loved one
> vacations or longer work holidays (How spent? Where and with whom?)
> fasting, certain food restrictions during special times
> sleeping, resting (When, how long?)
> other rituals or traditions

Then ask yourself and each other:
> How can we compromise on who does what, when and how often?
> Which activities do we each do alone and which together?

(16) Underlying values

Give examples of when either of the following seems more important to you than the other:
> the wishes and needs of a group or those of an individual
> spiritual well-being or material wealth
> relationships or the production of things/money
> the process or the end product

locks and boundaries or open doors
beauty or practicality; quantity or quality
relationships or cleanliness and order
saving face or honest criticism
handling one thing at a time or many things at once
When do you or don't you fight for what is right?
When and by whom is aggressive, loud interaction acceptable?
How is power shared or measured? by age, wealth, position, or — ?
When does admitting to failure appear weak? When strong?
Which of the following characteristics will help a person to survive:
courageous, self-confident, or passive and carefree?
cautious, suspicious, or trusting and determined?
aggressive, forward, or non-assertive and giving?
always friendly or serious?
Before exchanging answers with your partner, ask yourself the following:
What value differences have I noticed already?
Can I accept the different values of my partner?
Can we live harmoniously and in peace despite these differences?
Which of my values am I willing to change to please my partner?

(17) Worldview

Think about these questions and exchange answers with your partner.
Is man essentially good, evil, neutral or suspicious?
Does the spirit world control my life?
How do I view nature: to be respected, used or protected?
Which is more important and when: past, present or future?
How does my view of time influence the way I live?
What purpose does suffering have?
Can I know what is real?
What is real? Is what I can see or touch as real as what I cannot see or touch?
Am I really less or more important than, or as important as, my fellow man?
Are love, sacrifice, happiness and sorrow real or imagined?
Is this life I now have the only one I'll have, or is there more?

(18) Religious beliefs and morals

*Compare your views with those of your partner and note where you agree. Then
ask: How would our differences in these views impact our life together?*
If the spirit world or a higher being controls our lives, what is my role or
duty?
What do I believe about an after-life?

What are my beliefs about birth? Death?

What is my religion's attitude toward women? Toward the elderly? Toward family?

Who are my current religious leaders or source of authority? Do I follow them? How?

How do I rid myself of shame and guilt?

What is my responsibility toward others?

What rituals do I do when, how often, where?

How do my religious beliefs differ from yours?

Am I open to changing my current convictions about religion, or do I currently believe that I would never change them?

(19) Educational background and goals

Does my partner accept the educational standard I have achieved?

If not, what does he or she expect me to achieve?

Do I accept the educational standard my partner has achieved?

Is my partner open to seeking more education later on?

Would I encourage or support his or her educational goals for the future?

What would be my reaction if he or she failed or gave up?

(20) What makes me feel significant?

Ask yourself and each other, which of the following make you feel important:
present or desired career
social status or role,
talents, abilities, recognition and awards
being a member of my family
role or status in my family
role in a club, church or in the community
List some other sources of what would make you feel important in the future
future hopes, dreams, goals for me? (career, property, status, etc.)
future hopes, dreams, goals for my partner?
future hopes, dreams or goals for my children?
alternative plans in case these dreams do not get fulfilled?
if these goals are not fulfilled, what else could make me feel worthwhile?

(21) Governments and politics

Can you and your partner honestly exchange opinions without fear of being rejected or laughed at, or without being punished or put in danger?

Name or list some political issues concerning the country you currently live in, and find some which you and your partner agree on, such as,

types of government and political systems
political party of preference
the problem of poverty and the homeless
your country's attitude toward certain other countries
wars past and in progress, military service, nationalism
willingness to fight or die for one's political cause

(22) Engagement and wedding protocol

In your family, how is an engagement properly celebrated?
Do you or your partner want a legal contract regarding finances?
When is sex permissible or expected? Before or after the engagement, before
   or after the civil or church wedding ceremony, or — ?
What are some of the pre-wedding rituals in your culture?
If you were to marry publicly, where would it be?
Who and how many will you invite? Will there be a reception for all who
   attend, and/or another for relatives and special friends?
Who will pay for the wedding expenses? How much is the budget?
Which cultural tradition will dominate or how will both be expressed?
Which language(s) will be used? What music will be played?
Who dances with whom?
What physical contact will take place?
Will alcoholic drinks be allowed at the wedding?
How long will the couple have to stay with the guests or family?
Are any other customs or rituals expected?

(23) Who leads whom?

Currently, who leads in which aspect of your relationship and when?
How might this change if you changed countries of residence?
What is your expectation of your partner's leadership role or of his or her
   response to your leadership?
What is his or her expectation of your leadership role or your response to his
   or her leadership?

(24) Roles and routines: Who does what when?

Who is expected and allowed to work outside the home?
Who is supposed to do the heavy work (yard, lifting things, repairs)
Who is expected to manage the household, clean, prepare the meals?
Who is expected to teach and to care for children??
Who manages the cash for food and household shopping?
Who might earn more, and does it matter?

Who is to control the bank account, manage savings and other property?
Who is expected to initiate love making?
Who decides to move the family to another location?
Who decides on interior décor and furnishings?

(25) Money matters

How much (more) money do we need?
What material possessions do we want to acquire? How do we get them?
Why get rich or richer? to help others or to have more for ourselves?
Who might earn more, or does it matter?
How much does each set of parents help when needed?
Do we owe our parents — how much and with interest or without?
Who manages the household money?
Who gets how much pocket money?
Do we want joint bank accounts or separate or both?
Investment and savings: Who, what, where and for how long?
What does "ours" include — his or her family and clan?
What happens if you inherit something from your parents — is it ours or yours?
What happens to "ours" when one of us dies or leaves the marriage? Do the children automatically get the money, or does the spouse?

(26) Parenting and children

How many children do you wish to have? Gender? Names?
What do either partner's parents expect?
Will you use birth control? If so, which method?
Are you pro-life? In which case would you agree to have an abortion?
What religious ceremonies are to be performed in childhood? In adolescence?
Who will care for the children?
Who will discipline them? How?
Who chooses their schooling? Their careers?
What language will be spoken or taught?
Which religion will the children be exposed to and expected to follow?
How will you respond if the child does not conform to your hopes and expectations in regards to
religious faith and practice?
career ?
marriage?
place or future residence?

(27) Family influence and extended family issues

Discuss the following:

In what ways and to what degree are you and/ or your partner dependent on your or his or her parents or extended family …

   financially?
   career-wise?
   housing?
   emotionally?

How powerful is the influence of my/your parents in our joint decision-making?

Is a sibling dependent on either of us?

Who will care for the elderly parent(s) when in need?

How do we, should we, handle conflict with either of our parents?

What expectations do each of our parents, grandparents or siblings have of me? Of my partner?

(28) Things we enjoy doing together

Make a list of the things you and your partner enjoy doing together. Include goals, projects, people, activities, fun things, work, etc., and go out and celebrate doing them.

Refer to Appendix II "Personal Priorities of Choice."

Personal Priorities of Choice

In choosing a life partner, we all have our own unique preferences of characteristics we want our partner to have. Some are more important than others, and some are not important to us at all. This inventory can be used ...

- to see which (and how many) of the items you wish to be true of a partner are actually true of the partner you have or are considering

- to celebrate what you like or enjoy about each other

- to understand why you are (or are not) interested in this person as a life partner

How to use this inventory:

- Make a copy of this list (on the following pages) for your partner and let him or her follow the same directions below

- Check off or mark the items you think must be true or wish very much to be true

- Among the items you marked as above, underline or highlight the items that are very true or usually true

- Ask each other questions if either of you don't know

- Exchange what you have marked and discuss it. What you do then is up to you!

We strongly recommend that you do not attempt to look at, and discuss, all of the following lists at one sitting, but rather only a few at a time.

Communication and language

He or she ...

communicates in a way that I can understand most of what s/he says
likes my accent and accepts my language mistakes
is trying to learn my language
accepts my communication style (direct, indirect, loud, soft, etc.)
can talk about things that interest me
understands/accepts my humor
accepts the way I express my emotions
listens to me with respect and interest

Character, maturity

He or she ...

is self-assured, has realistic self-image, cares for own needs
respects boundaries and accepts the limitations of others
is a responsible member of his or her own family
is humble, teachable; consciously works on improving him or herself
accepts his or her own limitations and failure and tries again
can separate emotions from reason
separates parental influence from own thinking and other input
is honest (according to his or her cultural or religious standards)
abides by the rules and laws which he knows
is responsible in carrying out work assignments, keeping a job
is cooperative and attentive to others' needs
is generous, considerate, kind, forgiving, patient, gentle
is persevering, thorough and enduring
exercises self-control in stress, conflict, anger and frustration

Loyalty and fidelity

He or she ...

holds my viewpoint regards to life partnership and/or monogamy
pledges fidelity until "death do us part" and seems trustworthy
knows that I would leave him or her only if (?).........

Healthy stability and functioning

He or she ...

makes it a priority to maintain good health and a balanced life
has learned to cope and make the best of his or her limitations
seeks care and takes the appropriate medicine when needed

if affected by trauma in the past, is being treated for it
if psychotic or mentally disturbed or depressed, gets professional help
is not dependent on any illegal drugs
is not addicted to any other dangerous or unhealthy habits

Common interests and passions

He or she ...

likes to watch my type of movies or programs on television
enjoys watching the same sports with equal level of passion as I
has tastes similar to mine in music/art/ or literature;
enjoys doing at least 3 fun things or activities with me inside
enjoys doing at least 3 fun things or activities together outside
gives me the freedom to develop or maintain my own friendships
gladly allows me freedom to pursue my talents and interests
likes to travel and see places with me in our off-work hours or days, we
    spend more time doing things together than apart
enjoys or tolerates my pet (or the same pet that I would like to have)
has or wants a pet that I tolerate or enjoy

Values and worldview

He or she ...

is aware that there are differences in cultural values
is beginning to understand the culture that i come from.
listens to and understands my values and worldview
is aware of his or hers and can communicate them clearly
respects mine, talks reasonably with me about them and tries to compromise
    with mine
has experienced the "feel" of each other's country
knows what each of us value about our own country.
recognizes that attitudes to time, personal space and family reflect cultural
    values

If not the same religion or church membership

He or she ...

gives me the freedom to practice my religious activities
listens to my viewpoints with respect and an open mind
tells me his or her views without pushing them on to me
respects/accepts/tolerates my holidays and traditions
does not force me to participate in his or her religious rituals
allows our children to learn about my faith and religion

If same religious faith and church affiliation

He or she ...

shares the same views as mine

attends religious activities with me as often as I

enjoys the same faith community (such as church membership)

likes to talk about our faith with others to the same degree as I

applies his or her religious principles in daily living and relationships

Geography of residence

He or she ...

likes our current place of residence

has adapted well to the current place of residence

agrees with me on the preferred country of future residence

is aware of the legal restrictions of visas and citizenship

realizes possible reverse culture shock and my cultural adjustment if we
move back to his or her country

is willing to move to my country or spend time there in the future

Gender roles, power and influence, equality

He or she ...

accepts my level/ use of power/influence in our relationship

respects my leadership in some areas of expertise

shares the same view of gender roles regarding household tasks

agrees with me as to who manages the household finances

has same view as me regarding who may initiate or refuse sex

agrees with me on whose culture dominates our lifestyle

does not abuse power through threats or physical aggression

Respect for cultural tastes

He or she ...

likes my type of food and cooking

likes or tolerates the music of my culture

enjoys the art/colors/crafts and interior décor of my culture

does not ridicule or condemn my tastes or cultural preferences

is willing to give up some of his or her cultural preferences while living in
my country or in my presence

does not force or pressure me to give up one or my cultural preferences or
adopt one of his or hers

Conflict and potential conflict resolution

He or she ...
    can freely and openly talk out disagreements in a peaceful manner
    doesn't mind if I offer my viewpoint if it differs from his or hers
    can openly state his or her opinion that is contrary to mine
    is open to compromise, negotiate, and sometimes concede (give in)
    strives for a peaceful, friendly atmosphere despite disagreeing
    is open to using a neutral mediator when we fail to resolve a conflict
    apologies when wrong, asks for forgiveness and is ready to forgive

Intellectual/educational aspects and know-how

He or she ...
    shares approximately the same or similar levels of intelligence
    accepts my level of education as mine and is not ashamed of mine
    is not ashamed at his or hers if the level is lower than mine
    respects my goal of attaining a yet higher education or training
    strives for a higher education or training
    enjoys reading and learning about my culture and country of origin
    likes to learn new things as much as I do
    notices and respects my expertise, knowledge or talents

Security, compatibility on financial matters

He or she...
    is content with what he/she has, yet responsible
    is ambitious, responsible, disciplined and hardworking
    has a stable job or a career which I respect, or is trying to find one
    agrees, respects and accepts my career and job
    is financially stable, or manages money well
    strives to make more money without sacrificing important relationships
    will help pay the bills if we marry and have a family
    agrees with me as to who shares how much in the household expenses would
        want me to marry him or her although I own very little or nothing

Personality, stress management and life style

He or she ...
    likes my personality (extroverted or introverted; quiet or loud; etc) respects
        the way I handle stress, frustration, anger and past issues
    is not okay with my unhealthy life style habits and tells me so
    is trying to change his or her unhealthy lifestyle or habits

even if s/he doesn't change, I could stay with him or her

Physical appearance of the person,

He or she …
    notices the way I look, smell, walk, etc and compliments me often
    asks me to give input on dress, hairdo, etc.
    complies with my request or input
    lets me buy things that enhance his or her appearance
    doesn't ridicule me concerning parts of me I can't change
    asks me sensitively to change the things I can change
    offers to pay for changes I cannot afford or care to change
    pledges to accept me despite physical changes due to aging

Sexual attraction and behavior

He or she …
    asks me when and how I would enjoy his or her sexual touch
    welcomes and enjoys my sexual touch and indicates how and when
    expresses enjoyment in the way I treat him or her sexually
    does not force him or herself on me when I am not willing
    respects my need for sleep when I am too tired
    complies with my wish for the quantity and style of foreplay I enjoy
    understands the difference between my needs and his or hers
    is willing and open to talk about sex when I want or need to
    uses protection measures against unwanted pregnancy or sexually transmittable diseases

Acceptance and approval by others

    His or her parents accept me as a potential spouse
    My parents accept him or her as a potential spouse
    My siblings and extended family members accept him or her
    His or her siblings and extended family members accept me
    My society and broader community accept him or her (race, culture, nationality)
    His or her society and community accepts me (race, culture, nationality)
    My church or religious body accepts him or her as s/he is (faith).
    His or her religious body or church accepts me as I am (faith)
    His or her friends accept me
    My friends accept him or her

Career, type of job

His or her career or job suits my expectations/dreams/honor

I am not ashamed of his or her career or job

My family is not ashamed of his or her job or career

His or her family is not ashamed of my job or career

Our careers are compatible with each other in regards to time scheduling and the place where we live

S/he understands the stress or demands or dangers of my job and is supportive of me

We work together in the same business/firm/organization and are content doing so

We work in separate careers or jobs and are content working apart

Mutual trust, respect, support

I trust him or her and have no reason to mistrust him or her

S/he trusts me and has no reason to mistrust me

S/he respects me and treats me respectfully

S/he deserves my respect and trust

S/he is supportive of my goals, dreams and ambitions

I enjoy supporting him or her goals, dreams and ambitions

S/he is considerate of my special needs (shortcomings, challenges, weaknesses) and does not ridicule or shame me, and tries to help

His or her special needs are manageable to me

When s/he feels jealous, s/he behaves in a way I can accept

Social manners , legal matters

S/he is willing to learn and follow the social rules of my culture

I am willing to learn and follow the social rules of his or her culture

I am not ashamed of him or her when my family or friends are present

We can laugh and talk about our differences and are willing to learn

S/he knows and is ready to obey the laws of the land where we live or will live (if other than his or her home country)

I know and am ready to obey the laws of the land where we live or will live (if not my home country)

Responsibility toward the extended family

S/he knows and agrees with my family's expectations of me and my responsibility toward them (due to my gender or place)

S/he understands and agrees with the possibility of long-term hospitality or care toward members of my extended family

I understand and agree with the possibility of care and hospitality toward members of his or her extended family

S/he is not dependent on his or her parents regarding finances, life style, beliefs, etc., and if s/he is, it's OK by me

His or her parents or siblings are dependent financially on my partner, but I can accept that as long as it doesn't affect my security

S/he accepts my wish to keep close contact with my parents and siblings

S/he doesn't mind if my family and siblings keep in touch with me.

S/he has an amiable, peaceful relationship with both her/his parents

S/he has made every effort to resolve conflicts with family of origin

The relationship between her/his family and me is peaceful and friendly

View of marriage, history of marriage, divorce, wedding rites

S/he believes in marriage for life

S/he has never been married before

S/he was married before and it's okay with me

I have been married before and it's okay with him or her

I am sure that s/he is not presently married or engaged

S/he has no children from previous marriage or has them and it's okay

We have agreed to include something from each of our backgrounds in the wedding service

We agree on the type, place of wedding rites

We agree on a marriage contract

We practice and plan to practice safe sex to avoid STDs

Parenting and children:

We agree ...

on whether we want or don't want children, and if so, how many

on the use of birth control, how long and how

on the issue of pro-life and abortion

as to which religion and culture our children will be exposed to

that the children will learn the following language(s):

on what type of education our children will get and where

as to who would train, teach and discipline them, and how

as to the way we show love and affection to our children

as to who will be the primary caretaker(s) when they are young

as to which set of grandparents will care for our children

as to how our parenting style should compare with that of my parents or
with that of his or her parents

Age and age difference, illness, retirement and old age

If our age difference is significant, we are aware of the resulting cultural
differences (such as in taste of color, music, dress styles, or as in values,
religion and even worldview, etc.)

We are open to caring and providing for each other when one is ill or
physically dependent on the other (both genders)

We are open to various options regarding retirement — timing, place and
finances, his or her country or mine, and agree

When one of us retires, the other is prepared to adjust to the resulting
changes

Resource List and Further Reading

The following are additional ideas and sources of information which can be useful to a couple seeking to get to know their own cultures better and that of their partner:

o Travel books can be used as discussion starters.

o Books about culture written to help business people to succeed in foreign contexts are very helpful and can sometimes be found in other translations. Inter-cultural Press has a good selection of these as well as about particular countries.

o Novels or autobiographies or biographies.

o There are numerous websites on intercultural marriage, bi-national marriages, bilingualism, interfaith and interracial issues.

o Look for art exhibits, live theatre and movies and other cultural activities to experience together.

o Listen to world music.

Further Reading

Bennett, Milton J. 1998. *Basic concepts of intercultural communication.* Yarmouth, MN: Intercultural Press, Inc. ISBN 1-877864-62-5

Chapman, G., Bell, S., and Bell, D. 2004. *Five Love Languages Study Guide for Spouse and Group.* Chicago: Northfield Press. ISBN 10 1881273628, ISBN 13 9781881273622

Fraser-Smith, Janet. 1993. *Love across latitudes, a workbook on cross-cultural marriage.* ISBN 0 904971-05-8 (order through www.AWM.org/bookandvideobazaar)

Hampsden-Turner, Charles Trompenaar. 2000. *Building cross-cultural competence: How to create wealth through conflicting values.* New York: Yale. ISBN 0-300-08497-8

Hofstede, Geert. 1997. *Culture and Organizations: Software of the Mind.* New York: McGraw Hill. ISBN 0-07-029307-4

Hofstede, G.J.; Pedersen, P.B.; and Hofstede, G. 2002. *Exploring Culture: Exercises, Stories and Synthetic Cultures.* Yarmouth, Maine: Intercultural Press. ISBN 1-87-786490-0

Kohls, L.R. 2001. *Learning to think Korean: a guide to living and working in Korea.* Yarmouth, Maine: Intercultural Press. ISBN 1-87764-87-0

Lanier, Sarah. 2000. *Foreign to familiar: a guide to understanding hot and cold cultures.* Hagerstown, MD: McDougal Publishing. ISBN 1-581580-0223

Lewis, Richard D. 1999. *When cultures collide: Managing successfully across the cultures.* London: Nicholas Brealey. ISBN 1-85788-087-0

Paxman, Jeremy. 1998. *The English, portrait of a people.* London: Penguin Books. ISBN 4-026723-9 0

Pollock, D. and Van Rekin, Ruth. 2001. *Third Culture Kds.* London: Nicholas Brealey. ISBN 1-85788-295-4

Storti, Craig. 2001. *Old World, New World: bridging cultural differences.* Britain, France, Germany and the US. Yarmouth, Maine: Intercultural Press. ISBN 1-877864-86-2

Seelye, H. and Ned Wasilewski, J.H. 1996. *Between cultures: developing self-identity in a world of diversity.* Illinois: NTC Publishers. ISBN 0-8842-3305-6

Triandis, Harry, C. 1995. *Individualism and collectivism - (series: new directions in sociology).* Colorado and UK (Oxford): Westview Press. ISBN 0-8133-1850-5

About the Authors

Grete Shelling holds a Master's and an Education Specialist degree in counseling from Georgia State University and a diploma in pastoral counseling from the Psychological Studies Institute. She has many years of experience counseling couples and individuals in multicultural settings in both USA and Europe and has authored several articles on cross-cultural issues. Born in Austria, she and her family immigrated to North America when she was ten. She is married to Ted, an American. Together they have one grown son, and they enjoy personal and e-mail visits with friends from around the world.

Janet Fraser-Smith was born in England and immigrated to Canada at age 10. In her late 20's she returned to the UK where she met her English husband, Keith. Together they have worked in Egypt, Jordan, France, Cyprus and the UK, and she occasionally accompanies her husband who travels internationally in his work. She holds a B.S. degree and teaching qualifications. As author of *Love Across Latitudes*, a workbook for those considering a cross-cultural marriage, she has contributed to seminars on intercultural marriage in eight countries. Members of her extended family have lived for periods in 12 countries and five continents. Keith and Janet have three grown children and several grandchildren.

Printed in the United States
115673LV00002B/225/P